CALLED BY SPIRIT: BECOMING SARAH

A Spiritual Memoir of Light and Resilience

SARAH KRYGER

Published and printed in the United States of America.

While this is an autobiographical memoir that reflects with as much accuracy as memory allows the personal experiences of the author, some names have been changed to protect privacy.

Cover design by David Provolo
Editing by Sage Taylor Kingsley www.SageforYourPage.com

Hardcover ISBN 979-8-9998385-0-6
Paperback ISBN 979-8-9998385-1-3
eBook ISBN 979-8-9998385-2-0
First Edition

Published by Yawning Dove Publications
YawningDove.com
contact@psychicmediumsarahkryger.com

In Memory of My Mum

During the course of writing this book, my mum passed away suddenly. Life threw me a curveball, one I never saw coming. I found myself needing to pause and tend to my own grief. Just six weeks earlier, I had undergone a total hip replacement, and suddenly I was traveling halfway across the world while still healing—physically and emotionally.

Since her passing, I have come to understand not only my own grief, but hers as well. I can now see that at times she felt unseen, carrying her own struggles quietly. Through this journey, I have come to feel my mum closer than ever before.

One morning, I woke to the song "Alone Naturally" by Gilbert O'Sullivan, and I felt it as a message from her, a quiet reassurance that she, too, had known grief, had carried sadness, and that I would be OK. The song reflects the quiet reality of loss and the way we learn to live alongside it, rather than overcome it. In that moment, I understood that my mother had carried her own pain in silence, and that this experience of grief was not meant to break me, but to deepen my compassion, my understanding, and my soul's evolution.

Over the past ten years, and especially since my own spiritual awakening, our relationship had softened and matured. Though we had our struggles and differences, a deeper, more forgiving love grew between us.

There is still so much I wish I could say to her. Not hearing her voice or receiving her messages has been hard, especially at Christmas, and yet I strongly feel her presence, more easily in a sense, because I'm connecting with her soul directly.

As I continue to process my own grief with all its shifting emotions, I have gained a deeper understanding of my clients and what they experience. Grief has no beginning and no end; it simply is. We learn to meet it as it arrives, one day at a time.

I honor my mum's life and thank her for the experience of being her daughter. I am grateful for all she taught me, even through moments of despair and darkness, and for the love that continues beyond what can be seen.

This book is dedicated to her.

Gillian Greenall (1944-2025)

CONTENTS

INTRODUCTION

Welcome! This book invites you to walk beside me through the turning points that awakened my soul.

In the early chapters, I return to my childhood, where pain and intuition quietly took root. I didn't inherit my struggles; I faced them head on. Within the dynamics of my family, I learned how to stay quiet, how to survive. Later, a move roused something deep and unspoken within me, stirring a sense of destiny that I didn't yet understand.

The unraveling of old identities and relationships followed, the letting go of roles that I thought defined me.

And then the moment that changed everything: a grief that broke me open and became the doorway to my spiritual awakening.

Signs and synchronicities began to appear. A heightened sensitivity to energy. A language my soul began to speak without words. I share what it is like to develop psychic gifts—and how unsettling and beautiful this awakening truly was.

I am taking you into the transformative work of forgiveness. The power of remembering past lives. The way Angels and Guides make themselves known through sacred signs and whispers.

This book is not just a memoir. It's an invitation to remember who you are.

Let it meet you where you are. Let it wake something inside you.

There are no coincidences. Your journey has brought you here with for a divine purpose.

With All My Love, Sarah

CHAPTER ONE

Sarah Who?

It's fascinating how many of us end up in places that seem far from where we started, often leading to personal growth and new experiences. I believe that our life paths are shaped by a combination of choices, chance encounters, and a higher purpose. I am a perfect example of how a plan, set in motion before I was born, came together later—in my case, over the past four years.

I will use various terms for God, such as "Spirit," "Source," "Higher Self," and "Soul," but they all represent the same divine essence. I have come to understand that we connect with God in different ways, and these reflect my personal experience and relationship with the Divine. No matter the name, we are all referring to the same loving presence that walks beside us on our journey. There is no right or wrong way to perceive God.

I recognize, too, that my beliefs and how I perceive God reflect different stages of my life.

We are all interconnected; we are all energy. I now refer to "Spirit" to describe my connection, and at times, I will refer to my "spiritual team." Whatever terminology resonates with you, and however you access this higher wisdom, trust it and allow it to be your guide as spirituality is very personal.

I was born at 11:45 AM in the coastal town of Eastbourne, situated in East Sussex, England. I like to envision my birth as a remarkable event—a blessing for my mum and dad. Despite the hardships of my childhood that may suggest otherwise, I still hold onto this belief.

I was born with very little hair, a natural blonde. Looking back at the few childhood photos I have of my own children, I see a striking resemblance. At first, my parents called me Sarah Jean, which appears on my birth certificate, but it was later changed to Sarah Jane. I'm not certain why it was changed, unless it was due to a misprint.

My dad was Irish and Protestant, born in a small village called Cookstown, while my mum was British and Church of England, from Eastbourne. I remember my mum telling me that when they got married, my dad didn't allow her to invite any of her Catholic friends. What I understand now is that it wasn't really about belief, but more about control. Later in life, my dad shared that some of his cousins were killed by the IRA (Irish Republican Army).

My earliest memory dates back to when I was around three.

I vividly recall my mum changing someone's nappy, which is British for diaper. I remember feeling warm and excited about this little person I would eventually come to know as my sister

Tessa. This is the earliest happy memory I have.

My next memory is of lying on a couch; the fabric felt rough and harsh against my little face. As I was lying there, I heard an argument between my parents, then the sound of breaking glass as the TV was thrown through the front window. This would be the first of many traumatic memories.

Me at age 3

My next memory is from a couple of years later when I was out with my dad. At that time, my mum and dad were separated, so it must have been his afternoon to spend with us. My little sister, Tessa, was in the backseat while I sat in the front. I remember we took a drive to Beachy Head on a rainy afternoon, and I can clearly recall the white cliffs and the sea. I remember my dad's black hair slicked back, and when I think of it, I picture

The Fonz from *Happy Days*. Dad was a very handsome man who always smelled good.

Dad parked in front of a shop with a large window, which offered a clear view inside. I don't remember the make and model of his car, just that it was dark and had two doors. I remember the smell of the exhaust. Through the glass, I saw the shop owner, Frank, with whom my mum had been spending a lot of time lately, standing in the front window. The shop was on Seaside Road, just one street over from my childhood home on Sheen Road.

That day, back when I was only four, my dad asked me, "Sarah, is this where your mum's boyfriend works?"

I replied, "Yes," unaware of the consequences that would soon unfold later. My mum had made it very clear—almost coldly—that this information was not to be shared, especially with my dad. I remember the way she had looked at and spoken to me, her voice firm and unshakeable. There was no room for questions, only silence. I was afraid of her, and I felt like a child holding a secret too big for her hands. Yet there I was, doing exactly the opposite, without much thought of the consequences. We all know that keeping a secret is no easy task for a young child, especially when faced with a direct question or the strong desire to please others around them.

Later that afternoon after we returned home, a fight began. My dad confronted my mum about the new man in her life. Angry words were exchanged, and I remember feeling the walls close in around me, like the very air was being sucked out of the room. Terrified, knowing I was in serious trouble, I squeezed behind the same rough, itchy couch, covered my ears and waited. My heart raced as the argument between my parents escalated. I could hear things breaking, like china cups hitting a wall. I am not sure who was throwing what, I just know it was loud. I froze in fear and kept quiet.

My dad left the room. Suddenly my mum grabbed me roughly and dragged me out from behind the couch. Her fingers tightened around me, then she began to slap me. Those slaps were hard and directed first at my butt, but sometimes missed and instead struck my back. Her punishments often left bruises and welts, and I would carry the pain for days—and the emotional trauma for decades.

It was after that incident that I said my first prayer.

Crying my heart out, I asked God if He could please make it stop. This was not just a prayer; it was a cry for help. Even though my prayer didn't stop what happened that day, it planted a seed of faith that would carry me through many storms.

About ten months after that incident, my parents finalized their divorce. They had already been separated, and weekends were now spent with my dad. I still remember his small flat in Eastbourne's Old Town, on a narrow, winding street. He lived there with his girlfriend; her name and face long faded from my memory. What remains clear is the feeling of that place: a small bedroom filled with the soft glow of a lamp, and a double bed with soft bedding. Tessa and I shared that room when staying with him. It was in this place that some of my deepest childhood wounds were formed.

At age five, I experienced things that no child ever should: sexual assault at the hands of my dad. Though much of it has thankfully blurred over time, certain memories remain vivid—the smell of his aftershave, the sound of his breathing, and the heaviness of his body on top of my small one, along with confusion about what was happening to me. It continued for about a year. As you can imagine, this was very deeply traumatic, and I am still diligently working on healing that part of me that was taken at a very young age, my innocence. During that same period, I was still living through physical punishment at the hands of my mum. What a heavy load for a small child to carry!

Yet even through the agony of it all, I continued to pray and ask God for help.

Even though I still don't understand why I had to go through all that at such a young age, looking back now, I can see moments when I was protected. Situations that could have ended differently didn't. I was kept alive when I easily might not have been, and I believe now that God was with me in those moments.

Two years later, when I was seven, another frightening incident unfolded. My dad had recently been hired by a construction company based in India and was preparing to leave the country. His skills at operating heavy equipment were highly valued, and I have often heard people say he was so skilled with a backhoe that he could scratch someone's back with it. My dad decided that I should travel with him to India. My mum had full custody, with just the weekend visits to Dad as the only exception. Dad never contested that during the divorce proceedings, but now he wanted me to move to another country with him. My mum was not about to let that happen.

My dad repeatedly threatened to kidnap me, making demands on the phone, so my mum contacted the authorities. I remember one police officer stationed at our home and another escorting me to school and remaining there until the end of the day. This continued for several weeks as they tried to locate my dad. We learned later he was already in India, making many of the calls from there. He never returned to England or Ireland again, afraid of arrest and paying back child support, and instead relocated to Texas where he later remarried twice.

You may be wondering about my sister Tessa. Was she also abused by our dad? Did he threaten to take her to India, too? The truth is, I don't know. We never spoke openly about it. I do recall my dad once saying that he didn't believe Tessa was even his daughter. I couldn't understand that, as she looked just like him. I asked our mum about it once, and she brushed it off quickly: "Don't be ridiculous. Of course she's his." When it came to the kidnapping threats, those were only about me.

A few years after the divorce, my mum remarried. My stepfather, Frank, delivered milk for a living. He was nice to me and looked like Clark Gable. Soon, Mom gave birth to my littlest sister, Clare. I can still remember how adorable she was, full of light and joy. She brought a sense of softness into our home that hadn't been there before. But I also began to notice how differently my mum treated her. There was a tenderness in her voice and warmth in her touch. As a young child still carrying wounds, I couldn't help but feel a twinge of jealousy. I longed for that kind of attention too.

I suffered various forms of physical and emotional harm by my mum during my childhood. In fact, it's difficult for me to recall any moments when she showed me affection. She was always angry toward me. I always felt like I disappointed her somehow, which was a terrible feeling, actually worse than the abuse. The one thing I wanted most was affection, but instead, I lived in constant dread, wondering when the next outburst would occur and what I had done to deserve it.

I now believe that she somehow knew what was happening during my visits with my dad and that she blamed me for his overwhelming affection toward me, which he never showed to Tessa.

Before her passing, I repaired my relationship with my mum and came to truly love her, even though she never did acknowledge what I am sharing here. I hold no resentment toward either of my parents, as I later came to understand that both had faced their own traumas during their upbringings. While some might argue that this doesn't excuse their mistreatment of me, I realize that everything happens for a reason. I have been able to transmute abuse into healing and ultimately soul and emotional freedom, and I wouldn't have arrived at this point without those experiences—and the guidance from Spirit.

These soul connections were established before my birth, all aimed at helping my soul learn valuable lessons. This also taught me the transformative power of forgiveness and that each of us has a story of pain or hardship that we often keep hidden. I will delve deeper into forgiveness more in Chapter 10 and soul connections in Chapter 12.

Despite the emotional and physical pain I faced, there front and center were my mum's parents, who I fondly called Nan and Granddad. Oh, how I miss them! They were my rock, and I felt so much love when I was with them. I often tell people that they raised me, and in many ways, they truly did. Without them, I would never have experienced joy or what it felt like to be loved. Though this was a confusing and unsettling chapter in my young life, because of Nan and Granddad, I learned for the first time that there were people to protect me, when I was not able to protect myself, people who loved me unconditionally and reliably.

Every weekend, I would stay with them, soaking up any bit of love they offered. My granddad was a hardworking man, tall and lanky, while my nan was short, standing at just over five feet. She would often joke that as she got older, she was shrinking with age. I use that term now as I get older. She was a truly loving and kind soul and loved God; when in her presence, I felt grounded and anchored.

My family didn't attend church, so I only attended when it was required by my school, which, I believe, was standard for all schools in England at that time. Religion merging with education seemed normal to me. I'm not sure if this is still a requirement or if students now have a choice not to attend a church service. I loved God, and I believe my nan played a role in that.

My Nan and Granddad—1985

I feel my grandparents sensed that my home life was difficult, but I don't believe they were aware of what my dad had done to me. I never discussed it. I had tucked away those painful traumas into a corner of my subconscious and hidden the key.

My fondest memories are of watching my nan bake; she could whip up something delicious in no time, for example, Victoria sponge cake, or freshly baked blackberry and apple pie. Her date bars were my favorite. I've never been able to make them quite like hers. I was always allowed to help, just so I could lick the bowl or have the first bite.

My granddad enjoyed constructing things, tinkering in his shed, and taking walks along the beach with his companion: a part black Labrador and part Doberman who was just a puppy when my granddad adopted him. He named him Ghipy. I'm not sure where that name came from, but it was significant to my granddad. A name connected to his days in the Army. Ghipy was one of my best friends growing up, and I would now say that sweet dog was most definitely one of my Spirit Guides.

Ghipy and me. I was four years old.

Granddad in full regalia

Playing accordian with Granddad and Uncle Roy

Granddad and I frequently went on bike rides and sat by the beach to enjoy a flask of hot tea, along with a homemade scone. I loved the sea then, and I still do. I hold dear the sensation of the salt air on my face, and the scent always brings back memories of home.

Both of my grandparents had a fondness for birds, and my granddad had a particular love for canaries, which he raised and showed. I began showing canaries at age nine. We traveled up and down the East Coast to showcase them, and I won many ribbons for best in show myself. My granddad could play the bagpipes and performed with a military band; when he traveled, my nan would go along for the ride. He also played the accordion, which he taught me to play. We would often visit his younger brother, Roy, in Gilford and play for hours. I never considered myself very skilled, but I was good enough to win an award when I was about seven and continued to attend competitions till I was around ten.

Holidays were always celebrated at their home. My sisters and I would find presents on Christmas Day around the tree, or sometimes a special gift from Father Christmas was left outside our bedroom door to find when we woke up. I would often wake up in the middle of Christmas Eve to try to catch him in the act, but that smart Santa was onto us, and we never saw him.

At our own home, when we were younger, the three of us shared a bedroom. Later, as I got older, I was given my own room, and Tessa and Clare shared a room. It felt like a small rite of passage, getting my own personal space, even though it was just down the hall.

Christmas traditions in England are somewhat unique, featuring different foods and customs. One tradition I particularly enjoyed was opening presents hanging on the tree branches on Boxing Day, December 26th. And let's not forget the incredible food! I can still smell the roast turkey, filled with homemade stuffing, along with roast potatoes, parsnips, and brussels sprouts. Christmas pudding, drizzled with heavy cream, plus boxes of chocolates and homemade toffee. Christmas pudding is still a treat I enjoy, and even as an adult in the U.S., when the season would roll around, I would receive a package from my mum with not one but two mini puddings. YUM! Oh, how I missed those this past Christmas without her.

Playing nurse, around eight years old

Most of my childhood, I was kind of chubby, probably due to all those wonderful cakes my nan made, and I'm sure I ate to hide the pain. I have had issues with my weight all my life. Food always has been my go-to comfort or coping mechanism to deal with (or stuff) my emotions, instead of trying to understand why I am hurting.

School was very challenging for me. I had several learning disabilities, including dyslexia and what we now refer to as ADHD. I was paired with a teacher who offered extra assistance with reading and writing, and it helped me more than I realized at the time. Mostly I worked on my grammar and read aloud to build self-confidence, which really made a difference. But ADHD wasn't yet widely recognized, and I'm not sure it even had an official name back then. I think people assumed I was either not very smart, or lazy, or too distractable.

Because I was different, and very shy, it was like I had a target on my forehead and back, attracting bullies. I was bullied for most of my school years, not just by one bully but by many, every day, mostly by girls, although a few boys called me ugly. Those mean girls would pull my hair, shove me, and call me names, endlessly taunting me with fat jokes. Mostly, I felt the name calling was harder on me than the physical assaults, however, one day, I was pushed down the stairs—several times! I often came home bruised and battered. Once, I was intentionally hit on the head with a hockey stick during a game. I was knocked down to the ground and removed off the field. There was no escape from it and no help, either. I chose not to tell the teachers in fear of retribution. I felt they were aware and had seen this occurring on several occasions. I mentioned it to my mum a few times and even talked to my nan about it, but nothing was ever done. It was terrible. I felt incredibly isolated and didn't understand why no one was standing up for me.

I mostly kept to myself and spent most days alone; riding the bus after school felt like the worst part of my day. There were no school buses back in those days, just public transportation. I preferred the double-decker buses, where I could sit on the top level, but that turned out to be a mistake. It was more isolated, and it meant coming down the stairs, which made me feel even more exposed. Sitting on the lower level of the bus was a bit better, but even there I wasn't safe from unwanted attention. The kids that bullied me on the bus weren't strangers; they were in most of my classes. That made it harder. I had to sit with them through lessons during the day, then face their cruelty again on the ride home. They would corner me at the back of the bus, call me names, yank my hair, or shove me into the seat. Sometimes one of them would punch my arm or trip me as I walked by.

In those days, buses didn't have cameras; instead they relied on mirrors to see the upper and lower levels, and most of the bad behavior was easily missed. Now, of course, cameras are everywhere. Some days I'd get off the bus early and walk the rest of the way home, and other times I wouldn't take the bus at all, which meant walking five miles in the rain and the cold.

I even went so far as to call some of those bullies and ask if they would just stop and give me a little break. Can you imagine how humiliating that felt? Not that it made any difference, because the next day, they would be right back at it. As I reflect on those past days, I can still feel the emotions surfacing.

But despite the difficulties, there were good moments at school. I loved playing hockey and netball, which is similar to women's basketball. Our team made the newspaper a few times. When I turned thirteen, I began to change—physically and socially. I didn't have many friends, but one, Tracey, lived just a few doors down. We would hang out, sneak cigarettes, and sip some of her mum's cider. We felt pretty cool.

At fourteen, I discovered punk rock and instantly loved its sound and style. I began to smoke and drink more, and then all of a sudden, I began to lose some weight, which made me feel empowered, stronger and I dove headfirst into the punk scene. I started spiking my hair and dressing the part, wearing tight jeans and combat boots. Back then, punk rock was a big deal, and it became popular due to Sid Vicious of the Sex Pistols. I was more drawn to Siouxsie and the Banshees. I just loved Siouxsie Sioux's look and sound and still to this day listen to her music. Tracey and I listened a lot to Happy House along with any music by Toyah Wilcox. I especially loved "It's a Mystery" and "Thunder in the Mountains." With my limited funds, I would visit charity shops to piece together my punk look. I felt strong wearing this look. I knew I looked tough, and that was important to me. Too bad we weren't allowed to dress like that at school due to the strict uniform code, nor were we permitted to have pink hair. So, on the nights I hung out with other punk rockers, I would use food coloring to dye my hair. I felt cool, and I even pierced my own ears and eventually started piercing others' as I got skilled at it. My punk rock days are among my favorite moments in life.

I often reflect on those times and smile. I didn't care what others thought, including my mum. I began to stand up for myself. However, this rebellious phase sadly led me to lose interest in school; my grades began to slip, and I got into fights with girls who previously had been bullying me. Oh, how the tables had turned! Here I was, a tough punk rock chick, fighting back. Suddenly, I became a popular girl at school and mostly everyone wanted to be my friend.

I even caught the eye of a couple of boys, because I was considered *cool.* I finally embraced life a little more, hanging out with different people, staying out late, and fully enjoying my new identity. Something within me had undoubtedly shifted. I believe it was all part of my soul's plan.

With boys came a whole new set of challenges, because my early childhood traumas caused me to fear being touched. This wasn't surprising, really, but I wanted to fit in and was naturally affected by teenage hormones. So I was at odds with myself, wanting to kiss and sexually explore … but also feeling a repulsion I couldn't explain or change. My other girlfriends already had boyfriends and often bragged about their sexual encounters, while I didn't have much to share and felt like a late bloomer. In the midst of any make-out or heavy petting sessions, I would back out, due to fear of physical contact. I still struggle a little with anxiety around sexual touch today.

At seventeen, I met a young man my age who helped me open up sexually. Andrew and I had an instant connection, and I felt different around him. It took me some time, but he was patient and never pushed me beyond my comfort zone. When I finally let my guard down and allowed myself to experience a true connection, it was transformative. This was on my terms and with someone I felt safe with and connected to: my first love. Life-changing in every way. I would have married him, if he had asked, but he never did. I often wonder what my path would have been like if we had married. Where, and who, would I be now?

We dated for almost three years until he suddenly became distant, and I wondered if he was cheating on me. Ultimately, he decided he no longer wanted to be in the relationship, and I found out later that he had been fooling around towards the end. I blamed myself for possibly being too clingy. I truly loved him, and it broke my heart when we parted ways. I had no interest in finding another. Mostly due to feeling unsure about my body and that deep distrust again, I could not imagine being with anyone but him.

Andrew did end up marrying the one after me, and they had two boys together. My mum sent me a photo of their wedding day, featured in the local paper. As I looked at it, a wave of sadness washed over me, mixed with a bit of jealousy. I couldn't help but wish it had been me standing beside him on that day. Tragically Andrew passed away of a heart attack at age forty, and to this day, whenever I return home, I always visit his grave to say hello.

I now believe he was definitely a soulmate, someone destined to cross my path in this lifetime to help me come out of hiding and feel what it was like to be touched by someone other than my dad. Touched with kindness, healthy desire, and romantic love. Like with other soulmates in my life, we had planned this journey together before we were born. I once read that we experience three romantic connections or loves in our lives each shaping us in profound ways. If this is true, then he undoubtedly was my first, the one who taught me about deep connection and trust.

When I was twenty and Tessa was seventeen, both of us still living at home, we received an unexpected letter from our dad, who was living in Porter, Texas, married to a third wife. We both were a bit taken aback yet intrigued after reading it. The letter inquired whether we would be interested in traveling to see him; he would cover the cost of the flight.

Our mum was not pleased, and she felt insulted that we would even consider the offer. Tessa decided not to go, and she felt I shouldn't, either.

However, I didn't see it that way. I saw it as an opportunity to travel and visit my dad. You might wonder why I even considered seeing him after all those years, and after what he had done. But I had no memory of what had happened to me. I honestly didn't feel much emotion at all, just curiosity and a strong urge to go, so I said yes.

My granddad had fallen ill just after the letter had arrived but before I left for Texas. He suddenly started having more angina attacks and had a bad bout with stomach flu. This really took a toll on his health. Granddad became the focal point of my attention, and I put my trip on hold. I could not imagine my life without him and continually asked God to heal him. I looked up to him and valued his opinion. When I told him about my plan to visit my father, he looked directly at my nan then expressed that he felt I should go and discover for myself if that was truly what I wanted. I pondered that for a while.

Did my granddad possess a deep intuition? Or did he have some kind of divine insight? Nan was clearly battling with the idea. Neither of them thought highly of my dad because he had been a completely absent father and provided no support, financially or otherwise. But my granddad trusted me enough to go take that important trip and learn what I needed to, and most of all, he encouraged me to trust myself.

As I look back on my childhood, I see my experiences intertwined in both light and dark, with each one contributing to the strong woman I have become today. The pain and problems may have seemed incomprehensible at times, but ultimately led me to discover my resilience, strength, and faith in Spirit.

In the moments of darkness, I found hope. This hope was often nurtured by the love of my nan and granddad, the support of my friends during my teenage years, and the connection I forged with my first soulmate who showed me what love can be—all leading me to believe there had to be more to my life. These moments taught me that every obstacle is a steppingstone, each bringing me closer to personal growth. I am grateful for the divine intervention that guided me through tumultuous times, especially in my childhood, and for the moments when I turned to God, asking for help and finding solace.

I invite you, Beautiful Soul, to reflect on your own journey. Embrace the challenges, for they often lead to the most profound transformations. Remember that even in the depths of despair, love both for yourself and from others can illuminate the path forward.

Just as the stars shine brightest against the night sky, our spirits can emerge strong and radiant from the darkness.

Trust that you, too, are on a journey scripted by a higher purpose, and always remain open to the lessons it brings.

Open to my own lesson, not knowing what lay ahead, I made a bold choice.

I was going to cross the ocean. And see my father.

You are seen, you are worthy, and you belong.

Please also see the Appendix in the back of the book for uplifting affirmations for your heart and soul.

CHAPTER TWO

Threads of Connection

Every person has their own unique experiences, thoughts, and emotions that shape their identity, distinct from their parents. Many of us overcome difficult, unhealthy, or even toxic or abusive parental influences, demonstrating strength and autonomy in creating our own lives. Some of us spend decades trying to meet their expectations, attempting to prove that we've succeeded, to earn their approval. I especially wanted my parents to be proud of me.

What I am here to share is: *What you inherit from your parents doesn't dictate your future, as you have the power to change and evolve.*

After a long flight, I finally arrived in Houston, Texas. I could feel the difference in temperature. I had never experienced such heat before. I felt a mix of excitement and anxiety. Who was my dad now? Now twenty, I hadn't seen him since I was six and wondered if I would recognize him.

As I approached the end of the terminal, I noticed a man and woman standing to my left. The man appeared to be in his late 40s (he was forty-three). He had a deep tan and a heavier build, while the woman looked much younger, with a fuller figure and shoulder-length wavy brownish hair. I walked toward them, assuming it was them, and indeed it was my father and his third wife, Melanie, who, I found out shortly, was only a few years older than me.

A wave of nausea hit me as I began to doubt whether or not I had made the right decision. This was the moment I had been waiting for, and yet all I wanted to do was turn around and get back on the plane. But it was too late, so I tried to stay calm. I felt awkward as my dad leaned in to hug me. His hug was tight and left me feeling squirmy while his wife's hug was lighter, and yet a little tense. I sensed they were as nervous as I was. Even though I had no memory of my past encounters with him, I felt something was off. I never did get comfortable with him hugging me, though I couldn't pinpoint why. I just assumed it was because we hadn't seen each other in such a long time.

Why couldn't I remember what had happened to me when I was very young? And why did I even have to go through that? One might think that God would have spared me from such experiences, and I questioned that for many years. Now I understand that it was part of my greater purpose, propelling me farther on my spiritual journey. And I remembered just what I needed to, in divine time.

I don't recall much of our conversation on that visit, but I was excited to see his home and visit some places I had dreamed of. One was the set of the series *Dallas*. I was a huge fan, and it felt incredible to think that I was going to be there. I was also a big admirer of John Wayne. I had watched most of his movies growing up, and the thought of being in the USA, where he was born and filmed many of his movies, was thrilling beyond words. Years later, I visited where John Wayne was born in Winterset, Iowa, and I still have places on my bucket list like Ridgway, Colorado, where my favorite movie *True Grit* was filmed.

My dad seemed to enjoy showing me around. Melanie, on the other hand, appeared distant. I suppose I might have felt the same if my husband had invited his daughters from a previous marriage, and especially if one was close to my age. She never warmed up to me, and that dynamic persisted throughout our relationship. I always wished she could have been more of a friend than just an aloof stepmother.

About a week after I arrived, my dad took me to a service at his local Pentecostal church known as the Gospel Assembly of God. I had never been to a church such as this, and what caught my eye first was that all the women had their long hair up and were wearing dresses or skirts and long-sleeved blouses. Not a single one was in short sleeves, despite the warm weather. The men all wore suits and carried Bibles. Some ministers sat on the stage, including my dad, while only a couple of women were up there to sing and play the piano, including my stepmother. Looking back, I realize she had incredible gifts. Hearing her play the piano and sing in church was quite inspiring. I often wished I had the same talents.

This was also the first time I witnessed speaking in tongues—a practice associated with Pentecostal and Charismatic branches of Christianity. It involves the utterance of sounds and syllables that do not correspond to any known language, believed to be a holy language or a form of prayer. Those who believe in it view speaking in tongues as a gift from the Holy Ghost or Spirit, given to believers as a means of communication from God. It is often associated with deeper spiritual moments.

It was certainly eye-opening and inner-ear opening. Yet I felt so out of place. My hair was short, loose, and burgundy, I was wearing pants and a short-sleeved shirt, and I had no idea what I was seeing and hearing. My dad was watching me, I'm sure trying to see if I was going to freak out. But I kept my composure, even though it felt very weird and unsettling. While all of this was happening, I was quietly talking to God, asking Him to watch over me.

After the service, the congregation welcomed me warmly, asking me a lot of questions. I'm sure my dad had told them of my arrival.

The next amazing thing that happened was in the last few days before I was to return home to England. I encountered the power of the Holy Ghost personally! I was sitting on the side of my bed, feeling strange pins and needles, which now I feel as energy. I had a strong sense that I was not alone, that someone was with me. I had never encountered that before. Suddenly, I found myself speaking in a different language, feeling part of something much greater than myself.

Reflecting now, I sense that, along with the Holy Ghost, an angelic presence was with me. This marked the beginning of the next chapter of my soul's journey and capacity to channel holy words and sounds.

I now refer to this as Light Language, the language of my soul.

You too have your own unique light language.

The three weeks I was in Texas passed by quickly. Soon after I returned home, my granddad suffered a massive heart attack and didn't make it through the night. I remember receiving the phone call informing us of his passing. I was heartbroken. He was not just my granddad; he was like a father to me. He'd played a huge part in raising me and did so the best way he knew how, and I will always be grateful for that.

Trying to be strong for Nan and others took its toll, but I did my best to support those around me, even though I was struggling, too. Losing my granddad was truly a defining moment in my journey.

Not long afterward, my dad called, asking if I would come back and stay a bit longer. I agreed.

It wasn't easy leaving my family behind, especially my nan, but she encouraged me to do just that. I sensed she had an inner knowing that I needed to take this step to discover what I was seeking.

And what was I seeking? A deeper connection with God or with the Holy Spirit? All I knew then was that I felt a huge pull to head back to Texas. I had intended to be away only for three months, but now here I am today, thirty-eight years later, a citizen of the United States. I am grateful for my nan's strength in letting me go. I waved goodbye, boarded the plane, and headed back to Texas to find out what lay ahead of me.

You are held, you are nurtured, and you are never alone.

CHAPTER THREE

Texas—A Sense of Destiny

Life has a way of leading us exactly where we need to be, even when we don't realize it at the time. Looking back, I see how every choice, every moment of uncertainty, and even every hardship were all guiding me toward something greater. This next phase of my life was full of love, faith, and difficult truths and lessons that would shape me in ways I never expected.

Two weeks after returning to Texas, I had the chance to take a thousand-mile bus trip with a group of church congregants heading to Belle Fourche, SD, to help build a brand-new church, as the existing one was showing signs of wear and tear, and their congregation was growing. We were gone for only three weeks, but during that time, I met my next soulmate, Phillip, who later became my husband.

When I first laid eyes on him, to be honest, I didn't feel

much at all. He was around 5'10"—skinny and had very curly black hair. I was in fact a little jealous of all the hair he had as mine was fine and couldn't hold a curl! We were the same age, just a couple of months apart. He did not look anything like his dad who was with him, so I assumed he got his looks and hair from his mom. During a service, I noticed him up front accepting prayer to receive the Holy Ghost. As I sat at the back and observed, the ministers laid hands on him and all of them spoke in tongues. A wave of emotion came over me. It was so intense! Then suddenly, he too began to speak in tongues. It was like time stood still for just a moment.

After the church service, a member of the congregation introduced us. We didn't connect right away; he was shy, and I was a bit nervous. To break the silence, I made a few comments about his hair. He finally managed to crack a smile, and for the next hour we talked mostly about where I was from and how n English girl like me ended up in Belle Fourche, SD. Within an hour of meeting him, I really liked him and felt good around him.

We spent a lot of time together over those three weeks, talking, laughing, and getting to know each other. One night, we stayed out way longer than expected, which sparked some concerns from the women I was traveling with. They came knocking at his apartment around 2 a.m., worried about where I was. But to be clear, nothing happened between us, aside from some heavy kissing.

There was no doubt I was falling in love, and the feeling was mutual. It didn't take long for juicy gossip to travel through the church community. All eyes were already on me, but now they were on us, the hot topic. Honestly it was probably the most exciting thing the church community had experienced in a while. I'm pretty sure this found its way to my dad's ears.

Over the next three weeks, the construction of the new church steadily took shape; it was much larger than I'd imagined. I stayed busy in the kitchen, preparing meals along with fellow church sisters, and it really felt good to be a part of something. I discovered a deep appreciation for helping others. It brought a sense of fulfillment. There were at times nearly fifty tradesmen volunteering their time. Phillip, who worked professionally as a painter, played a key role in the interior construction.

His father, a businessman, provided much of the financial support for the project. Much later, I learned that Phillip's father had had some questionable financial dealings with certain individuals, and he was not quite the man he appeared to be. In fact, those shady dealings had helped fund the construction of the church. When the church leadership eventually found out, they immediately cut ties with him. To me, this felt like an act of hypocrisy because who among us has never made poor choices? However he acquired them, he was directing those funds for good. His dad has long since crossed over, and despite the shadows of his past, he had a generous heart. He was at his core a good man when it came to helping others.

When the time came to leave, it was incredibly difficult to climb back on the church bus and head back to Texas. It felt like the end of the world, and I spent most of the trip in tears. I recall the final day of our journey when a handful of us, me included, fell ill with stomach flu. That was as unpleasant as life can get, especially while traveling. Back in Belle Fourche, several others also became ill, including Phillip.

Back in Texas, the months following my trip to Belle Fourche brought their own set of emotional and financial burdens. I was deeply homesick, especially missing my family and the comforting presence of my nan, as well as the loss of my granddad. On top of that, I couldn't legally work without a permit, which meant I had to rely heavily on my dad for support. Even though I never really asked him for much, at times I felt like a burden. That hadn't crossed my mind before I'd decided to make this second trip over. It's something I still catch myself doing leaping into decisions without fully thinking them through.

My newfound love was more than a thousand miles away, and the separation weighed heavily on my heart. Still, we stayed connected the best we could and talked on the phone for hours at a time, mostly about how we couldn't wait to see each other and about what our lives looked like moving forward.

Meanwhile, my dad was becoming increasingly distant. I often wondered if he regretted his decision to bring me over. I also sensed that my stepmother was growing weary of the situation. I imagine that must have been hard for her; after all we were only a few years apart in age, and I must have felt like an intrusion, certainly a competitor for his attention.

I learned that my dad had another child with his second wife, a boy named Jim, who was just nine when we first met. He lived with his mother (my father's second wife), and my dad had him on the weekends. I wasn't quite sure what to think of Jim at first. The age difference between us was significant, and discovering I had a younger brother threw me for a bit of a loop. I really did try to bond with him, but our relationship never became more than an acknowledgment that we were brother and sister.

Though I knew she was aware of my brother Jim, I wasn't sure how much my dad had told Melanie about my sister Tessa, or even about me and his marriage with my mum. Did Melanie truly understand what she was stepping into? Did she feel overwhelmed by the reality of it all, my dad having had three children with two former wives? These were questions I never asked and answers that were never offered, but I felt tension in the air all the same.

To take my mind off my emotional distress and longing, I knew I needed some kind of distraction, so I asked my dad if it would be OK to take the yellow Volkswagen Bug out for a drive around his neighborhood. I had taken a few lessons back home, but in England, of course, we drive on the opposite side of the road and everything in the car is set up differently. The steering wheel, the gearshift, even the pedals felt foreign, and I had to constantly remind myself to stay on the right side of the road. It was fun at first, and I felt I was getting the hang of it … until I accidentally hit the gas pedal instead of the brake. I did some real damage to the car and the garage wall. Yep, I crashed right into it. Yikes!

My dad was mad, and in his Irish-Texan accent spoke strong words. I can still hear his voice even now. "How could you be so stupid? That's the last time you will ever drive my car!"

That really was the last time I got behind the wheel of his yellow Bug, or any vehicle he owned. In fact, I never drove again until I was back in Belle Fourche with Phillip a year later.

After that ordeal, a wave of panic washed over me. I felt ashamed, inept, completely lost at times, yearning for home and the comfort of my nan. But even though I was deeply homesick, I let my plane ticket home expire. I wasn't sure how to tell Mum and Nan, but part of me believed they already knew I would not be coming back on that ticket. Because as much as I longed for home, a bigger part of me longed for Phillip, curious about where that relationship might lead. And I felt a strong pull to continue my Texas spiritual experiences, an inexplicable sense that I was meant to stay. Letting go of my return ticket only intensified the isolation I was feeling, yet I knew I was meant to stay and trust the process. A deeper part of me sensed that something greater was at work.

I began to strengthen my relationship with God, clinging to prayer, seeking guidance on how to find my way through. At times I still felt trapped, with nowhere to turn, and the weight of my emotions was too heavy to share with my family, so I held it in. I became morose and withdrawn.

One evening, Melanie got the idea that I was possessed by an evil spirit and that they needed to lay hands on me to cast it out. "Laying of hands" was something I had seen in church frequently. It seemed like every service, *someone* had *something* that needed to be cast out, except I never thought that someone could ever be me. What could I possibly be possessed with? Why? How?

They restrained me and laid their hands on me, praying and speaking in tongues, sometimes sitting on me and tightly holding my hands and feet. It was horrible, and an overwhelming sense of terror washed over me. I couldn't fight them off. I endured this for over an hour until they believed they had cast the evil spirit out.

I couldn't shake the feeling that they took some satisfaction in what they were doing to me. It deeply tested my faith and left me questioning the concept of evil spirits and the supposed need to cast them out. Having watched many horror movies in my lifetime, *The Exorcist* stood out the most, and that's exactly how I remember the experience, minus my head spinning or spewing green at everyone. Afterward, I was so shaken, I didn't speak for days. I kept to my room and did my best to stay unnoticed, afraid that it might happen again.

Just two weeks after the exorcism, my prayers were answered when Phillip asked if he could come visit me. After spending a few weeks together in Texas, we realized we didn't want to be apart from each other, and we decided to get married. There was no formal proposal; it was more of a mutual understanding, a shared certainty that we were meant to be together. And I was also ready to leave Texas and my dad's house behind.

After we got engaged, Phillip and I traveled back to South Dakota, where we planned to marry. I stayed with his grandparents, both preachers, for a few months before we exchanged our vows. Since our church upheld strict rules which forbade any intimate relations before marriage, the wait seemed endless, but we remained committed.

On Valentine's Day in 1987, in our church at Belle Fourche, we finally said: "I do." About fifty people attended, mostly fellow church members and a few of Phillip's family. My dad and stepmom did not come. I had hoped my dad would walk me down the aisle, but the excuse he made was that he couldn't get away from work. That deeply hurt. In the end, it was Phillip's grandfather who gave me away. He was a such a kind man, and I loved being around both him and Phillip's grandmother. The wedding was simple but sweet, nothing over the top, the meal was modest, and our cake was beautiful—until someone moved it, and it fell to the floor. That was the end of the cake.

I hadn't noticed the weather until it was time to leave the church, and by then one of the worst winter storms was howling outside—one of the biggest they had had in a long while. It was one of the first real snowstorms I had ever seen. The snow was coming down so heavily that cars were buried in about a foot of snow, and the roads were nearly impassable.

After the men did some digging, we climbed into Phillip's old 1979 Cadillac. I was terrified! It was not in the best shape and only had two-wheel drive. The defroster did not work, so we had to keep the windows rolled down just to see the road ahead. It was a slow, nerve-racking drive through the storm, and I remember praying and gripping the seat all the way home. What a relief to finally pull up in front of our little upstairs apartment in Spearfish, located just fifteen minutes away. Snowstorms are a way of life in that part of the country, and even though since then I have seen my fair share, that one still stands out as one of the worst.

My spiritual journey unfolded like a winding road, leading me from one ordeal to another for twenty-five years. Each one tested—and boosted—my faith, resilience, and sense of self.

You are on the right path, and the signs are all around you.

CHAPTER FOUR

From Toxicity to Triumph

The next twenty-five years were filled with sadness and loneliness for both of us. Looking back, I see how those years were shaped by choices we made earlier in our marriage. We moved to Houston, Texas, where we joined a church of the same denomination and lived in an apartment above the church. Phillip took on side jobs as a painter, while I stayed mostly in the apartment since I was unable to work without proper documentation, a green card which didn't come through for another ten years. Somewhere along the way, my paperwork had been lost, and with it many important documents such as my birth certificate and marriage license. I spent hours and hours on the phone with immigration and never got anywhere as they had no record of me. I was in limbo.

It was a crushing feeling, not being able to provide for myself, to feel self-sufficient or even capable of caring for my own needs. Strangely, those same documents resurfaced a decade later after Senator Larry Pressler of South Dakota helped set the process back in motion. But in those early years while I waited and hoped, my world remained very small. The only time I really saw other people was at church. My dad would stop by now and then, but over time his visits became less frequent.

I knew when we got married that Phillip wanted to start a family as soon as possible. Deep down, I had reservations, and to be honest, I'd never really thought about becoming a mother. I was OK with the idea if we chose not to. But I felt pressure from Phillip and others in the church, as if it was my duty. About a year later, our daughter, Jillian, was born.

Her birth was incredibly difficult. I originally had a midwife, but due to my high blood pressure during labor, I had to be transferred to a doctor, who didn't seem to have any patience. I had chosen not to have an epidural and instead used the Lamaze method. Thankfully, Phillip was permitted to stay in the room with me during labor, coaching me to breathe, but he wasn't permitted in the delivery room. I ended up in a room with six other women, all in labor at the same time. At one point, I even witnessed a set of twins being born, while still enduring my own labor.

After my water broke, it took another two hours before Jillian was finally born. I had pushed so hard and for so long, the blood vessels under my eyes burst. Later, I was told I had pushed beyond what my body could handle and created a pressure so intense, they broke from the strain! I looked like something out of a horror movie.

It was a grueling experience, and after Jillian's birth, I didn't even get to hold my baby! And to this day, I still don't know why I was denied those sacred moments. I missed so much, her first feeding and a chance to bond, to stroke her, to breathe her in. Watching my daughter cradle her own newborns after birth reminded me of what I missed, not just with Jillian, but both my children. Spiritually, I now understand those missing moments were a part of a greater path, one that would lead me here. To healing. To remembering. To writing this book.

I had to experience that aching absence so I could hold space for others who have felt unseen in their own silent grief.

Three years later, while living in Dallas, Texas, our son, Jason, was born, but he had serious complications. He had fluid in his lungs and was septic and immediately admitted to the ICU, where he remained for three weeks. It was an incredibly emotional and frightening time as a mother. The one piece of hope we held onto was that his weight was almost ten pounds; the doctors said this likely saved his life.

Jillian and Jason

Because HIV was a major concern during that time, Jason was given blood from a close friend for safety. Watching my newborn from behind the glass of a tiny cubicle, unable to hold or comfort him was heartbreaking. All I wanted to do was to bring him home. When that day finally arrived, it was one of the happiest moments of my life. My beautiful baby boy was finally back in my arms. Thank you, God, for carrying us through!

Even though we dearly loved our two children, there were moments when my husband was very withdrawn, and I struggled immensely with emotional turmoil and often felt suicidal. I wondered if I would ever get out of that relationship alive. Shortly after we got married, he presented signs of narcissism, which I honestly didn't understand much about until later. I felt he had a tendency to be very cruel and had a talent for inflicting emotional pain effortlessly.

I'm not perfect at all, and I brought my own set of emotional traumas to the relationship, just as he did. I could get very angry and sometimes even slapped him, something I'm not proud of.

The cruelty continued for years with Phillip. For instance, when I was thirty, and our children were eight and five, I became severely ill with double pneumonia from complications of the flu. I was literally on the verge of dying. Phillip was aware of how sick I was, but his primary concern was how we would pay for a doctor's visit. At the time, I couldn't even stand and had to crawl to the bathroom. I also suffered from intense headaches and severe pain in my legs, caused by a lack of oxygen. This lasted for three days, and I can only imagine how our children felt seeing me in that condition. Finally, he broke down and took me to a clinic.

I'm not sure how I managed it, but I walked into the doctor's office and sat in the waiting room. I was led into a small room, and I remember sitting on the floor because I could no longer stand. My husband sat in a chair casually reading a magazine. He never spoke to me at all. When the doctor entered, he immediately provided me with oxygen and rushed me away for X-rays. After the X-rays, I returned to the room in a wheelchair. The doctor explained to my husband that I needed to be hospitalized, or I could die. It was as if my healthcare was my husband's decision to make, not mine. I didn't realize the inherent misogyny and sexism in this until just now, while writing this.

My husband coldly rejected the doctor's recommendation, instead asking if I could be sent home with oxygen and medication. His words cut deep, and I felt forsaken. Totally unloved. Unworthy.

I begged God for answers, questioning why I was facing such hardship and cruelty. The ache in my heart was overwhelming.

We ended up going home with an oxygen tank, antibiotics, something for pain relief, and a promise that we would return the next day for a follow-up. While the oxygen provided some help, there was no way I was going to get better without serious intervention, and the doctor knew that.

The following day, I had more X-rays.

This time, however, the doctor didn't return me to the exam room. Instead, while in the X-ray room, he placed his hands on my arms and said, "Sarah, you are very ill and *need* to be in the hospital." He told me that the Muppet creator, Jim Henson, had died of double pneumonia, and that the same fate awaited me if I didn't receive *immediate* hospital intensive care.

I made my own decision and agreed to be admitted.

My husband declined an ambulance that my doctor had ordered and said he would drop me off, which he did. When I arrived, a team of nurses whisked me away. The first couple days were touch and go, but I was in good hands. God hands.

I had one profound moment when I closed my eyes and could see a tunnel with a white light at the end, a phenomenon often reported by those who have near death experiences (NDEs).

I asked, "Am I returning home?"

A soft-spoken voice replied, "No. It is not your time, Sarah."

When I opened my eyes, I was calm and felt an overwhelming sense of love from God. Something inside me had shifted. I felt comforted. A deep sense of security that there is more beyond this life, more than the physical body, and that I was being watched over. Embraced. Protected.

That moment quietly validated something I could feel but did not have words for: that God exists, that I was meant to stay, and that my life had a purpose, even if I could not see it yet.

After that, I began to improve significantly, but it still took some time to rebuild my stamina. They kept me in the hospital for eight days.

When my voice was strong enough, I called my mum to tell her I was very ill and uncertain about the outcome. She and, my stepdad George arrived within the week to help me recover when I got back home. They stayed three weeks. It took months to regain my strength.

I rarely think about that anymore, yet as I write this, intense emotions flood in. I realize that what I battle with the most is the lack of emotion and care my husband showed me. Now that years have passed, I realize that he truly didn't know how to respond to me being that ill, and that was simply how he coped.

After five years, my husband and I made the difficult decision to leave the church, realizing it was no longer aligned with our beliefs or the path we wished to follow. Stepping away was both liberating and unsettling; it forced us to redefine our spiritual identity outside of the structured faith we had known. Yet, this transition was just the beginning of a much deeper transformation—one that would take decades to fully understand.

One essential lesson I learned from all that was the lasting impact of what I have lived through. I connected the dots between my past wounds and the emotional distance from my husband, and this highlighted how unresolved feelings can linger and affect our present relationships. Acknowledging and expressing our emotions is a crucial step toward healing, as it can lead to deeper self-understanding and the ability to communicate our needs more effectively.

Twenty years after arriving in the United States, I finally became a U.S. citizen. The path to citizenship was long and winding, full of setbacks and complications. While my paperwork was lost in the system, without Phillip's support or willingness to help, the process remained at a standstill. There was little I could do because I wasn't a citizen yet. Looking back, this was one of the ways he maintained control over me, by keeping me dependent, unsure, and limited in what I could do. Ironically, it was a letter from his father to our senator that set my citizenship in motion.

On May 20th, 2007, I found myself standing in a room in Sioux Falls with 200 other immigrants from all over the world, all of us ready to officially become part of this country where we had made our home. It was a defining moment. When I raised my hand and took the oath, I felt a sense of belonging, a feeling of freedom, like I had finally closed another chapter in my life and started a new one.

Spirit kept urging me forward. After that NDE in February of 1998, I felt I had a strong sense of divine guidance and support. I continued to take one step at a time. Following my inner compass, I found myself on an entirely unexpected path as a radio DJ. It started on a whim. One night, I called the Top 40 station Hot 93.1 FM to ask about a song, and the DJ (who happened to also be the station director) asked what I did for a living. I shared that I was DJing at a local roller rink, and to my surprise he said he had an overnight on-air shift open and offered me the job.

That's the night Queen Sarah was born, my on-air name that soon became real. What began as a chance opportunity grew into a twelve-year career in radio across three different stations in Rapid City, SD. That gig led me to more shifts, and eventually, I was doing midday while also working as promotions director and music director. After almost seven years there, I moved to the Classic Rock station KSKY 95.1 FM where I was working on air on both the morning and midday shows for nearly three years, occasionally slipping in a song that carried a little more edge than the playlist allowed. My last stop was the Oldies station B101 FM where I hosted the midday show and served as both music and promotions director.

After years on air hosting shows, directing music, and leading promotions, I felt ready for a new chapter.

That transition came when I accepted the position as the event coordinator for the Deadwood Chamber of Commerce, in Deadwood SD. I worked diligently, spending seventeen years in that position, which brought out my creative side. What I genuinely loved was we all came together each of contributing in our own way. Watching all the pieces fall into place, from planning to execution, was deeply fulfilling. Having the opportunity to work alongside all city departments was also a pleasure, and we brought each event to life with energy, imagination, and a whole lot of teamwork.

It meant a lot to me that people trusted me, because they knew I was dependable, well-organized, and always followed through. My work proved that, and even though I am introvert, I enjoyed being with others, which at times meant mingling with thousands of tourists. When people ask me what my favorite events were, I always say Oktoberfest. I especially loved organizing the Wiener Dog Races and the Beer Barrel Games, both of which I created. They brought so much joy and entertainment to the community.

I also became known for the elaborate, imaginative costumes I created for Deadweird, an annual Halloween event held in town. The streets would fill with every single costume imaginable, and the creativity of people brought to life each year never seemed to amaze me. Even though I managed the event, I always found a way to design something fantastic for myself that would take months to finish. Each year I challenged myself to outdo the last. I couldn't officially enter the contest, but in my heart, I always felt like a winner, especially when people would stop and take photos of me.

I also built incredible floats over the years. My personal

favorite float by far was Falkor, the giant dragon-dog from *The Never-Ending Story.*

I remember my daughter saying, "You'll never be able to pull that one off, Mom."

Falkor is ready for the 4th of July parade.

Deadweird 2021 – Mother Nature

But I proved her wrong, and it turned out exactly as I pictured it. I still have Falkor in storage, and I bring him out now and again for parades. He never fails to turn heads and spark smiles.

I know this creative work was part of my soul's journey, shaping my growth, building my confidence, and allowing me to express myself joyfully. Over the years, I organized seventeen major events, each one filling my heart with purpose and pride.

As I poured creative energy into my career, both of my children, Jillian and Jason, grew into their own lives. I wasn't the kind of mother who made costumes or lingered over crafts, I was often stressed, overwhelmed, and short on time. Most of my creativity was reserved for my work, which demanded it. Still, my children were a part of that world with me. Even though by the time I was working at the Deadwood Chamber of Commerce, they were teenagers, busy with their own worlds, they helped with events that I hosted, building haunted houses, working on parade floats, and lending their hands and ideas. Love showed up not in elaborate gestures but in persistence and showing up even when I was exhausted.

They attended local schools, and each faced their own challenges; both struggled with dyslexia and ADHD, which made their school years far from easy. But they were strong-willed and determined, and I was proud of their resilience. Jillian was the first to move out, followed by Jason not long after.

And so began my quiet wrestling with the empty nest. It was an emotional shift, coming home to a quieter house, learning how to fill, or make peace with, the silence. Phillip was working out of town often, and our marriage was fizzling. I missed our children being around. Eventually, both kids returned home at various times, each for a season, before moving back out again, as life called them forward.

I found comfort in the unconditional love of my three labradors: Sunny, Tarney, and Dallas. They were more than just pets; they were companions of the soul. After my long days at work, they greeted me with such exuberant joy, offering a steady warmth that helped fill the emotional gaps.

Phillip's job took him out of town mostly every week, returning on weekends. While he was away, I had a bit of an emotional reprieve. It allowed space for me to breathe, reflect, and simply be. Little did I know that momentous change was on the horizon.

One day, while walking the dogs along a trail outside of town, I found myself having a very honest conversation with God. I remember asking how I might learn to accept my path, find peace with where I was, and solace in the love that still surrounded me. I didn't always hear answers in those scared moments, but I always felt heard. There was such comfort in knowing I wasn't truly alone. I had my work, my faith, and the overwhelming, steady love of three labradors who seemed to understand more than words ever could.

That moment sparked the shift that had long been needed. Something inside me changed, I felt stronger, more courageous. I realized I didn't need to stay with Phillip. Neither of us was truly happy. Even our children weren't surprised when we finally chose to part ways.

So, I took the first step and initiated the process of an amicable divorce.

Toward the end of my marriage to Phillip, I received a remarkable gift from Spirit: my next soulmate, Albert.

When I first met Albert, we clicked right away. I had just started my job in Deadwood as the event coordinator, and he was the parks supervisor at the time. Since we collaborated on events, we had plenty of opportunities to work together and our connection was immediate. At the time I was still married to Phillip, and Albert was in a relationship as well. Even so, our friendship began to grow naturally, built on shared conversations getting to know each other a bit better. There was always a sense of ease between us, and I felt a strong closeness, though I was never quite sure how he felt about me, other than that we were friends and colleagues. I simply appreciated having someone I could trust and talk to.

About five years in, I suggested we grab a drink after work. It felt casual, just two friends catching up, but then our conversation changed. As we talked, Albert shared that he had loved me for a long time. I was completely taken back and had no idea he felt the same way I did. It was a beautiful, tender moment, one that still lingers in my heart. I often look back on that evening, still amazed by how effortlessly it all came together, as it was always meant to be.

Albert and I had been together a few months when my divorce from Phillip was finalized. There was no contest from either side, and the process was surprisingly smooth. I believe it brought a sense of relief to both of us. Still, a part of me grieved the ending of our marriage. I was closing the door on a significant chapter of my life, and I could feel the weight of that within me.

Thankfully, my children seemed to accept Albert, and he welcomed them with an open heart. Though he had no children of his own, he embraced the role of stepfather the best way who knew how. About six months after our divorce finalized, Phillip remarried, perhaps a sign he had truly been ready to move on.

Albert was truly worth the wait. Our bond marked a profound turning point, not just in my life, but his as well. For the first time, we both experienced being deeply seen, valued, and genuinely loved. I'm not saying that Phillip and my children didn't love me, but there was and still is a special kind of joy in this partnership, something sacred that touched parts of me that I hadn't known could heal or come back to life. I had spent so many years feeling unseen, unwanted, or unworthy.

Through his eyes I felt seen. And I began to see the best in myself.

Through his love, I felt wanted.

Through our connection, I finally believed I was worthy.

My relationships over the years were complex, some painful, others loving, but all were part of my growth. I stayed in some places longer than I should have, often trying to hold everything together for the sake of the family. In the process, I lost parts of myself, slowly learning that love should never mean losing your sense of identity or your voice.

Keep going forward. Trust that everything is falling into place for you. You are a blessing, and the most important person in your life is *you*. You deserve the very best that life has to offer. You just need to believe in yourself and know that you are worthy of love.

Everything is possible for both you and me. You are not alone in your struggles, and there is purpose behind your experiences. We are in this together.

You are rising, you are reclaiming, and you are powerful.

CHAPTER FIVE

My Beloved Sunny

Sunny, a black Labrador puppy, came into my life just as I was nearing the end of my radio career. Phillip, the kids, and I had decided it was time to add another dog to the family, partly for us, but mostly as a companion for our other Lab, Tarnie. I spotted an ad in the pet section of the local newspaper. Someone in Nebraska had six Labrador puppies for sale. It was a bit of a drive, but we loaded up in our minivan and made the trip. When we pulled up to the house, I immediately saw the puppies in the front yard, chubby little things tumbling over each other, tails wagging and full of life.

It didn't take long for me to pick Sunny. I instantly felt he was the one. From the moment I held him in my arms at eight weeks old to the very last time I said goodbye, I knew there was something truly special about him. We developed such an amazingly deep bond. He loved me unconditionally, as I did him, and he supported me through difficult times by bringing me joy and showing me love. He was a gift sent to me by Spirit.

My beloved Sunny

Sunny was five when I began my relationship with Albert, and he adored him. But Sunny would always be my boy and the one "thing" I felt truly belonged to me. He was my furry companion, and I wouldn't let anything or anyone take him away from me. If he and Albert didn't like each other, I would have chosen Sunny, hands, er, paws down.

He was one of my soul connections, far more than just a pet, even more than an Animal Totem or Spirit Guide. Throughout the fourteen years he was in my life, Sunny was my source of comfort. I would often sit with him and talk about my day. He loved to play ball and swim, and although he wasn't much of a hunter (much to Albert's disappointment), he was an avid swimmer and ball catcher. I did, however, teach him, when he was seven, to kick the tennis ball back to me. Who says you can't teach an old dog new tricks?

I also trained him to sit and wait for my command, which proved helpful when I entered him in an event called Dock Dogs. Sunny loved the ball and water, so getting him to leap into the air, grab the ball, and land in the water was never a problem. The challenge was getting him *out* of the pool because he loved it so much! He never won an award, but it was such a delight to watch him.

In the last couple of months of Sunny's life, I began to notice that he was really not himself. He was not only facing bronchial issues, but his age made it difficult for him to get around, especially up the stairs. Deep down, I knew I would have to make that tough decision, but it's never an easy choice. I think we all would prefer to let them pass peacefully in their sleep, but unfortunately, that is often not the case, and we must help our furbabies find rest.

A week before his passing, we took a walk behind our home, which was perfect for hikes and connecting with nature. As I watched him walking very slowly on the path, pausing often and in pain, I knew it was time. I wanted at least a few more days with him, so I made an appointment with our vet for the end of the week. I spent those days pampering him, showering him with treats, and sitting with him for long periods, talking and enjoying our time together. Most of all, I made sure to show him love, so much love. He returned that love, and I felt he knew we would be saying goodbye very soon.

To this day, that remains one of the hardest decisions I had to make. The day we said goodbye, the weather was warm, and the sun was comforting. I had taken the day off, and even though I tried hard to trust that this was the right decision, when we arrived at the vet, I experienced two panic attacks and felt completely overwhelmed.

We had to wait for about an hour due to an emergency the vet had at the last minute. I remember sitting on the floor with Sunny, desperately trying to keep from having another panic attack. When the vet finally arrived, I got Sunny nestled in his favorite blanket and held him. When the time came for him to cross over, I still felt an overwhelming fear of letting him go, and yet I trusted he was in good hands, knowing that Spirit would take care of him, and that he would be reunited with our other family members, both furry and human.

We said our goodbyes and he was gone. As I write this, I'm overwhelmed with emotion and deeply miss him. Our furry friends may be with us for a relatively short time, but the impact they have on our lives is immense, and the pain of their absence is a testament to the depth of our love for them.

Throughout our years together, Albert and I have had to say goodbye to several of our beloved furry soul companions. Each held a special place in our hearts, and their presence in our lives was an incredible blessing.

Tarnie, a rescued Labrador and gentle giant at over 110 pounds, also graced us for fourteen wonderful years. Dallas, our beautiful champagne-colored Labrador, was full of love and personality but left us at age eleven due to complications from a stomach virus.

Our two German Wirehairs, Reba and Koko, were exceptional hunters and cherished members of our family. Reba passed from bladder cancer at age twelve, while Koko's sudden departure at age nine from undiagnosed liver cancer was especially heartbreaking. Despite regular vet checkups, we had no warning, and within three hours of an emergency visit, she was gone. Losing a beloved pet so suddenly, without the chance to say a proper goodbye, is gut-wrenching.

The bonds I shared with each of them were deep and meaningful. I miss them dearly, yet I am profoundly grateful for the time we had together. Their love, loyalty, and companionship were gifts beyond measure, and I will always treasure the memories we created.

All our furry companions are gifts from Spirit, reminding us how precious their lives are. Despite the heartache, Spirit reminds us to treasure the time we have with them, for as long they choose to stay with us. All relationships, including those with our pets, are divinely orchestrated, serving a greater purpose in our lives.

Though Sunny is no longer physically by my side, his spirit remains ever present. I still feel his love in the quiet moments, and I see glimpses of him in our black Labrador, Duke.

Love, after all, does not end. It simply transforms, continuing to guide us in ways both seen and unseen.

Sunny's passing was not just an ending but a beginning: a doorway to deeper understanding and spiritual awakening. Through the love we shared, I learned that the connection between souls, human or animal, never fades. We carry them with us always, in the spaces of our hearts where love resides eternally.

And so, I move forward, carrying his memory, his love, and the lessons he left behind. Sunny was, and always will be, one of my greatest teachers.

You are loved beyond time, and love never truly dies.

CHAPTER SIX

Spiritual Awakening

A friend once said to me, "You're having a spiritual awakening."

I replied, "Spiritual what?"

I truly had no idea what that meant or what it involved.

So, what is spiritual awakening? When you look it up, there are many different meanings, such as heightened awareness, sensing a greater connection to the whole (unity, oneness), questioning beliefs, and desire for growth. These are just a few common aspects, but overall, a spiritual awakening is a deeply personal experience and can manifest in various ways.

Over the past five years, since Sunny's passing, I learned what it meant to me, and quickly.

Only my Higher Self can explain why I was meant to learn as much as I could while stepping into my true self and calling.

It certainly has been a path filled with deep heartbreak, radiant joy, unforgettable experiences, turning points, and deep healing.

But ultimately, it has been about *discovering love for myself and remembering who I am as a soul.*

I have yet to meet anyone who claims that their spiritual awakening was easy. Nothing has shaken me more or carved me so deeply into who I'm meant to become. When Sunny passed away, I fell into a deep depression and found myself in a dark place with very little light. I grieved intensely, finding it hard to cope with daily life. I managed to mask my feelings quite well, but inside, I felt like I was dying.

While the losses of both my nan and granddad were undoubtedly difficult, this loss resonated on a fundamentally different level, catalyzing a more intense and personal sense of sorrow. I understand the reasons now, but at the time, I had a tough time seeing anything clearly … until an acquaintance mentioned a hypnotherapist who had provided her with amazing sessions. I didn't know what that entailed, so I had to look it up. A hypnotherapist is a skilled professional who uses hypnosis as a gentle therapeutic approach to help clients enter a state of focused relaxation and openness. This special state of consciousness can make it easier to explore memories, emotions, and thoughts that might be hard to access in their everyday waking life. I had no idea that this existed, but I found it very transformative.

My first session was incredibly emotional. Initially, I thought there would be no way I could enter a hypnotic state, but to my surprise, I did. My subconscious was able to hear everything while my conscious mind was busy searching for answers. As I went deeper, I started to see myself in a new light. I began to feel a sense of hope.

While my conscious mind was searching for healing, asking if my beloved Sunny was OK, I experienced a visitation from Archangel Gabriel. My soul recognized him. It felt like a vision, sudden and undeniable. I saw someone standing in a field of radiant light, their silhouette glowing, yet familiar. Though I couldn't see every detail, I knew in the deepest part of me that it was him.

His presence was commanding yet gentle, and when he spoke his voice was soft, but it carried a strength that pieced through everything It wasn't just a message, it was a call. Something within me was activated.

Although I don't recall our entire conversation, I vividly remember him telling me:

"It's time to remember who you truly are."

What a profound statement to make!

So, I began to ask myself, and still do: *Who am I that I need to rediscover?*

This was a divine gift bestowed upon me and the first of many to come.

The remaining hypnotherapy sessions were equally empowering, but that session changed me forever as I began to remember who I truly am: *A beautiful soul with gifts from Heaven.*

Yet another gift: My hypnotherapist, Tracy, became my closest friend, and our paths crossing was meant to be. We began our spiritual awakenings around the same time, and she has been my rock, as I have been for her, both supporting each other throughout our spiritual journeys.

Not long after the sessions ended, I began to sense things around me in a completely different way. There was a moment when I felt an intense tingling in my body and had the realization that I was not alone. During some of these divine tingles and downloads, I would gasp, unsure of how to express what I was feeling.

These sensations intensified. Then one day, while walking on the treadmill at our local gym, I noticed someone I recognized from the community. In that moment, I heard a faint child's voice. I wasn't sure if it was real, but I kept hearing, "There's my daddy, I love my daddy."

I could actually see a little girl, in a red dress; she was flying a kite or holding a bunch of balloons. She was not alone; a boy older than her was standing by her side. Initially, I brushed this off as my imagination, but for the next two weeks, I heard those words every day that I was at the gym and near that same man. I'd never experienced anything like this before.

He worked in public service, and I knew his young daughter had been courageously battling a serious illness for more than a year. She was only two years old, yet had already endured more than many face in a lifetime.

Our community rallied around the family. I attended a few fundraisers held in her honor, each one rooted in love and hope. One was meant to help the family take a special trip—something joyful, something magical—so she could experience a place she loved and meet a character that brought her comfort.

When she passed, the loss rippled through the entire community. She was deeply loved, and many prayers were whispered for that little girl, whose light touched so many hearts.

It had been a few years after her passing when I began working out at our local gym, where I would often see her father. We often shared a few words about life and how things were going. I never imagined that one day, I would be the one to bring forth a message from his daughter. I often reflected on his loss and how profoundly it must have affected him. His unwavering strength spoke volumes, and I couldn't help but feel the weight of his grief.

And now his little girl was reaching out from across the "other side." I could feel she wanted to communicate something to him, through me, but I had no idea how to make that connection. Here I was, still trying to acclimate to the idea of hearing those in Spirit.

So, I asked Spirit for a sign to confirm that this was real and whether I should relay the message. Within a couple of days, I had a dream where I was holding a sick child in my arms. That was my sign.

The next day, I began my usual walk on the treadmill, waiting for her dad to arrive, and wondering: *How am I supposed to approach him? How will he react? Will he even believe me when I say I have this gift and that his daughter had a message?*

I asked Spirit for courage and approached him. I told him about this gift I had and mentioned that I had been hearing his daughter for a few weeks. I explained that I had asked for a sign and had received one in a dream.

I asked if it was OK for me to share the message from his daughter. I always feel it is important to ask permission before sharing something of a spiritual nature, because some people are not ready to receive the information, and we need to respect their boundary.

His expression warmed, and with gratitude, he replied, "Yes! I'd love that!"

I went within, tuned in, and as I listened to her little voice, I shared her words—a message of love and forgiveness: "Daddy, I love you. And I know how much you have carried. But none of it is yours to hold. I'm with you, I've never left. I am at peace now.

Please don't worry. I love you so much!" As her words flowed through me, I felt her energy. So pure and innocent.

With tears in his eyes, he thanked me and gave me a hug. I had tears in my eyes, too, and felt so honored to serve as a channel, or what I now know is called a *medium*, one who hears spirits who have passed on and can convey their messages to their living loved ones. I am so grateful to have been chosen to deliver the message. Every day, I am thankful for moments like these.

The entire experience was nothing short of remarkable—receiving and conveying her message with such clarity, and my unshakable trust in its truth and origin. This, along with subsequent similar experiences, highlighted the immense healing potential of sharing divine messages. It reinforced the importance of trusting myself and trusting Spirit.

Additionally, it serves as a reminder that *grief can transform into something positive,* offering a sense of closure and a continued connection with our loved ones.

My life was changing. The decision of whether to tell Albert about my gift felt like a constant weight. It wasn't about his belief; it was the vulnerability of revealing a hidden part of myself. One night, as I lay in bed, I decided to share the story of the little girl with my husband.

I was unprepared for his response.

"You're a seer."

Those words changed everything.

What on earth is a *seer*? Albert explained that when he was in school, he'd learned about a world-famous trance medium named Edgar Cayce. He suggested I read about him, as it might help me understand my gift better. I certainly didn't expect that!

He was right. Learning about Edgar Cayce ignited my search

for deeper insight into what was happening to me, and it opened up a world of understanding. I highly recommend reading about him; he was phenomenal.

Edgar Cayce's abilities were extraordinary, earning him the title of the "Sleeping Prophet." One of the most fascinating stories about him is his claim that as a child he could absorb the contents of a book simply by placing it under his pillow while he slept. By morning he would know everything within its pages as if he had studied overnight. Intrigued by this idea, I once tried it for myself, but to my disappointment it didn't work. He was also known for holistic healings, often suggesting dietary changes, meditation, and natural remedies.

The term "seer" refers to someone believed to have the ability to gain insight into events, situations, or truths not immediately apparent just via the five senses. This often implies the capacity for clairvoyance, intuition, and/or the interpretation of spiritual messages. Seers are typically associated with prophecy, divination, and spiritual guidance and may use various methods, such as visions, meditation, or heightened awareness, to access knowledge about the past, present, or future. Some can even do remote viewing and help find lost objects or even people or solve crimes and other mysteries. In many spiritual traditions, such as shamanic practices or in the Bible where some prophets were considered seers, these individuals were highly regarded as having a special connection to the divine and spiritual realm.

I now understand that I walk the path as a seer, connected through Spirit and called to share what I receive with others.

I believe that we all possess these amazing qualities and more; each of us has incredible gifts. Isn't that amazing?

I quickly became a member of Edgar Cayce's Association for

Research and Enlightenment (A.R.E.). I am still a member today, and I have a photo of the headquarters location at West Virginia Beach on my vision board as a place I would like to visit.

I explored everything I could find about him, immersing myself in topics such as: trance mediums, psychic mediums, intuition, Spirit Guides, and Angels. I read about meditation, hidden meanings in finding a feather, Animal Totems, angel numbers, and synchronicities. Some concepts didn't resonate with me. I trusted my inner guidance to determine what I needed to focus on, and what I could just skim or skip.

What stood out to me most were the symbols and signs, because they felt like breadcrumbs left by the Universe, gentle reminders by my unseen companions. Feathers are frequent signs for me, offering me comfort and clarity along my spiritual path. (See Chapter 13 for more about feathers.)

This feather I found on my She-Shed.

Found while out walking on a trail, shaped like wings.

Everything I resonated with was really a reflection of my soul and what I needed to remember for my future spiritual journey.

Just over two years ago, I connected with a young woman who I now consider to be my soul sister: Ashley. She conducted a stone energy session, harnessing the power of stones and crystals to clear my energy. I highly recommend it, as stones are incredibly powerful in their own right. After placing the stones on and around my body, Ashley left the room, and as I laid there, I began focusing on setting the intention for healing.

During that time, I had a vision of two children, an older boy and his younger sister. I even received their names. They had died tragically in a house fire in the 1800s, somewhere out West, based on how they spoke and what they were wearing. I realized that this was a past life I was witnessing—but it wasn't mine. When I asked Spirit to explain, I was told this was a past life of Ashley's, and she was their mother! How amazing is that?

When Ashley returned to check on me, I shared what I had experienced, and let me tell you, the energy coursing through my body was intense, and the feeling of not being alone was ever-present. Overwhelmed with emotion, she felt the deep connection to these two children, her children from long ago. It made me ponder the essence of a mother's love. Does that bond ever really fade, even across lifetimes?

After that session, Ashley introduced me to Psychic Medium Dani Jo, with whom she was sharing an office. I was extremely nervous. I worried that a psychic might sense something weird … or uncover a hidden secret.

Dani Jo was standing in the doorway of her office, and as I walked towards her, I began to feel intense energy and an overwhelming presence of Spirit, which I was told was Archangel Michael.

I said, "Someone is here."

Dani Jo asked, "Who?"

I replied, "Michael."

She confirmed, "Yes, I felt him, too, by my right ear."

This part of my journey deepened my understanding of my own abilities and marked the beginning of my exploration into what that meant for my future and my next steps. Spiritual awakenings are just the beginning; they represent the tip of the iceberg when it comes to understanding who we truly are.

Our past lives connect us to aspects of ourselves that remain unhealed or from which we need to grow. They can reveal unresolved issues or traumas that are crucial for personal development.

Recognize the bigger picture and embrace your own gifts from heaven.

We are all interconnected with the Universe.

You are awakening, you are expanding, and you are Light.

CHAPTER SEVEN

Is That Ringing I Hear?

As soon as I began writing this book, I felt compelled to include a section on ringing in the ears. The medical term is *tinnitus.* Some individuals experience it in one ear, while others have it in both. I have it in both ears; it's more prominent in my right ear, but it's definitely present in both.

What I learned is that ringing in the ears may also be connected to Spirit. I share this with you because it took me some time to understand why I have ringing in both my ears. Even though I have come to grasp the reason behind it, I still occasionally feel anxiety due to it, and on some days, the ringing can be quite loud.

It began in March of 2022. I had started meditating every evening, and I really enjoyed listening to monks singing, which helped me relax and connect with Spirit. I initially thought the ringing was actually linked to the chanting. That night, I went to bed as usual, expressing my gratitude to Spirit for a good day.

In the middle of the night, I woke up to an intense ringing so loud it caused me to jump out of bed and triggered a panic attack. I ran downstairs, pleading with Spirit to tell me what was happening and asking if my Guides could make it stop. I ended up in my "she shed," a space Albert built for me across from the house, my personal sanctuary. A cozy 10' x 10' retreat beneath a Black Hills Spruce. He built it entirely from scrap wood and leftover materials from past projects, giving it a rustic charm.

A large window at the front allows just enough light, while a smaller window on the side lets in fresh air. I filled it with all the things I loved, infused with the echoes of memories of the long past: Sunny's footprint in plaster that the vet had made after he passed. A drawing I had done of him hanging on the wall. And representations of the blessings in my life today. I always have loved birds, so my space was filled with bird trinkets, each a small tribute to their beauty and presence. There were a few candles upon a small shelf where I also would burn sage to fill this sacred space with a sense of peace and quiet reflection.

That particular night, with my ears ringing so loudly, the noise was deafening. I entered my shed, shaking uncontrollably. Kneeling in front of the winged floral chair, terrified, I pleaded with Spirit for guidance and help.

Amongst the intense ringing, I heard a voice tell me, "Just breathe."

I began to recall the Lamaze techniques I had learned for labor, which have come in handy many times throughout my life. The power of breath is truly remarkable. So, I rose from my knees and sat in the chair. Still overwhelmed by gripping fear, I began to focus on my breathing, one breath at a time, gradually calming down and feeling more grounded and in control.

I kept hearing the message, "Just breathe." This continued for a few minutes, and then, suddenly, the ringing stopped.

Still feeling very emotional, I returned to the house and climbed into bed on my husband's side, seeking comfort. I told him I'd had a panic attack, and he held me for the rest of the night. In the morning when I awoke, the ringing had returned, but it wasn't as intense. It's a strange experience to suddenly go from silence to constant noise; even now, many days I miss the silence.

The next six months were tough. I couldn't escape the ringing. I kept asking Spirit if it was ever going to go away. I read extensively about tinnitus and even visited an ENT (ear nose and throat doctor), who couldn't find anything wrong and prescribed anxiety medication. I did my best to adjust to the constant ringing, but there were days when all I could do was cry, sometimes uncontrollably. It consumed my life.

I reached a point where I needed to sleep with background noise, like the sound of a running creek. I purchased a headband with earphones to help me sleep at night. I also started taking prescribed sleeping pills, which helped me fall asleep, although they didn't necessarily keep me asleep. I ended up sleeping in another room for a while because I had so much sound playing in the background that it was overwhelming for Albert at first. Thankfully he has since gotten used to the sounds of creeks or rain in the background and enjoys it.

I asked God daily when this might end and prayed for help to cope with it. A part of me sensed it might never go away, while another part desperately hoped it would. My spiritual team was busy and made several attempts to get my attention, but I wasn't really tuned in as I was consumed with this ringing, and it's harder to be intuitively tuned in when we are having strong emotions like fear, anxiety, or sadness.

One day during this period, I was having coffee with Tracy, who was aware of this issue. She told me she had come across a video discussing ringing in the ears, mentioning a potential spiritual connection. After our coffee, we stepped outside, and I smelled lilacs, which struck me as odd since it was the wrong time of year for them. I asked her if she could smell them, and she said no. The significance of that moment wasn't clear to me at first, and yet it was definitely a sign that Spirit was trying to communicate.

Following that day, I began watching videos, listening to podcasts, and reading everything I could about the topic. Eventually, I came across a couple of valuable sources, including a clip by Dolores Cannon (see Resources section at end of book) that explored the connection between ringing in the ears and Spirit, explaining the significance of each ear. Yes, each ear holds its own meaning! The right ear is more associated with connection, while the left ear is where we might receive a "download" or message, prompting us to pay attention to what's happening in the moment. It was all incredibly fascinating.

I began to shift my thinking and started paying attention, asking my spiritual team various questions about my experiences. I came across an article about a sound pillow that featured built-in speakers, originally designed for veterans with PTSD but now available for anyone. While it wasn't cheap, I felt it was worth a try to help drown out the ringing at night. It was life-changing! I have since recommended it to others. I now even have a travel version, and I never leave home without it. (See Resources for the website.)

I started to realize that this was now my life. I learned that the ringing in my right ear serves as my direct line to Spirit and my spiritual gifts. Although the ringing in my left ear is less intense, when I receive a message or download, it can feel quite overwhelming.

For example, recently, I experienced a profound download. As I drove back from a retreat I had been attending, a flood of insights came in, which I felt was the beginning of a book about my life. About fifteen miles from home, afraid of losing my thoughts, I pulled over and began to record them using my phone, capturing the ideas before they slipped away. Later that evening, I suddenly felt a loud high-pitched ringing in my left ear. The intensity was overwhelming, causing me to feel quite ill and triggering a panic attack. Although it lasted just a few minutes, it was enough to stop me in my tracks. Throughout, I communicated with Spirit, and eventually, the ringing faded away, though my ear was physically sore afterward. I called Tracy, and she helped me calm down and focus on my breathing. Even now I can find myself feeling emotional, worried that the sensation will continue.

This has changed my life. I am very sensitive to loud sounds, whether it's a band playing or a lawnmower, so I try to protect my ears with earplugs. I also discovered that I can ask Spirit to tone it down if it becomes too intense, and this frequently works, and the volume decreases. For someone who experiences constant ringing like I do, any help is greatly appreciated.

During that time, I had thoughts of suicide because I just couldn't stand it anymore. I had heard a news story about a man who developed ringing in his ears after contracting Covid. He ultimately took his own life, and I found myself wondering if that could be my fate. I worked hard not to direct blame toward

Spirit, but part of me was angry at God. I wondered if I was being punished and didn't feel I deserved it. I learned that it's OK to experience anger, as I felt it many times. No emotion is wrong; it's better to acknowledge and process it rather than suppress it. I will share more about suicidal thoughts in another chapter, as this is actually something that stems from my past lives and makes sense to me now.

Although this was a dark time for me, it marked my journey toward understanding what it all meant and transitioning from despair to hope. This duality is important, as it emphasizes that *even during difficult times, there can be moments of clarity and insight that foster personal growth.* All of this pushed me farther along my soul path.

One of my favorite quotes by Byron Katie, a well-known author and speaker is: "It is happening for me, not to me."

Fortunately, the ear ringing did not signify an end for me but rather marked the beginning of trusting Spirit and recognizing that it's OK to ask my spiritual team for assistance.

I now view my ear ringing as a gift and my direct line to Spirit. It reminds me of the quote from E.T.: "Phone home." I can reach out for help whenever I need it. I've also learned that it's essential to embrace all emotions, trust the healing journey, and remain open to the signs from Spirit.

Now, the ringing is part of my daily life, and my sound pillow has become one of my best companions. Occasionally, I like to add some background noise, such as monks singing, simply because I find it comforting. As I continue to navigate my spiritual awakening, I look forward to sharing even more of my experiences and insights in the upcoming chapters and quite likely, further books as well.

In the next chapter, we will explore an unusual perspective about "growing pains." They're not always what you think they are….

You have a direct line to Spirit,
and you receive divine messages.

CHAPTER EIGHT

Growing Pains

When my children were little, they occasionally experienced random pains all over their bodies. Whenever I asked my doctor about it, he would say there was nothing to worry about and that it was just growing pains. He would often inquire if their appetite had increased, and the answer was yes. So, growing pains are indeed a real phenomenon.

Currently, I have four grandchildren ranging from ten years old to four months. When my own kids mention that their children are complaining of pain, I suggest it might be growing pains, but I always encourage them to have it checked out by a doctor. It's somewhat like teething and can be uncomfortable, but it's a necessary part of their growth.

Growing pains are very real during a spiritual awakening, too, affecting not just the spiritual aspect but also the emotional and physical. Here are some of the growing pains I have experienced and continue to face, which might resonate with you. These are not necessarily in order and can literally happen at once or even in combination.

Emotional Turmoil: As you awaken, you may confront deep-seated emotions, past traumas, or unresolved issues, leading to experiences of grief, sadness, or anxiety. How true this is! The emotional upheaval can be intense at times. I often wonder: *How much more do I need to heal?* Just when you think you've healed from one trauma, you discover a whole list of others waiting for your full attention. Or a whole new level or layer to process and heal.

Overwhelming Sensitivity: You may discover that you are more sensitive to the energies, emotions, and surroundings around you, which can be both enlightening and draining. Empaths for example, often absorb the emotions of others without even realizing it, like walking into a room and suddenly feeling sadness and anxiety that isn't their own. I've experienced this many times myself, but over the years I have been more mindful and guarded. I do lapse now and again. Then add menopause into the mix, and I could become quite a challenge to be around—just ask my husband! I would cry all the time, and even now, my emotions feel very tender. I'm continually working on creating personal boundaries and being conscious of who I allow into my life because everyone has a different energy, their unique energy blueprint. I've become very attuned to that.

Isolation and Loneliness: You may feel disconnected from those around you as your beliefs and interests evolve, leading to feelings of isolation. This has been very true for me; even though I was busy at work and often surrounded by thousands of people during events, I still felt isolated and lonely. I felt different, and although I may not have shown it to others, the weight of it all was very real for me. Even though I love social events, I am an introvert and would prefer to spend my time at home in my she shed, yet this, too, can feel like a different kind of loneliness, longing for belonging. Not sure where I belonged anymore, at times I felt awkward, disconnected, and alone.

Questioning Relationships and Setting Boundaries: You begin to re-evaluate your connections, with family, friends, or work relationships, and consider if they still serve (or ever really served) your higher purpose. This has been and still is difficult for me, as I am a people pleaser and dislike hurting others' feelings. Yet, during my career as an event coordinator, I had to learn when to set limits and how to speak up for my own desires and needs; if I didn't, people would take advantage of me. I was never rude, just firm.

Discomfort with Change: Change is often uncomfortable, and letting go of old beliefs, habits, and relationships can be quite testing. I wrestled with the notion that if I didn't follow directions or do as I was told, I would be punished, and I found it particularly difficult to break away from old beliefs regarding religion. Some of this stems from my childhood, while other aspects seem to be rooted in past lives.

Searching for Meaning: As you awaken further, you may find yourself wrestling with fundamental questions and seeking deeper meaning in life. This quest for deeper truths is both enlightening and evolutionary, because it inspires more authentic reflection and expression of who you are now. Awakening souls yearn for a profound way to make a difference. This is because we are attuning more with our God-given purpose, our mission on Earth. And we ask deeper, philosophical questions, no longer just accepting what others have told us, no longer settling for a status quo that is not aligned with personal meaning.

Physical Symptoms: You may experience physical sensations like energy surges, ringing in the ears, or changes in sleep patterns or even shifts in your libido, either heightened or diminished, as your body adapts to new levels of awareness. I have encountered all of these and more. I discovered that pain in my body often indicates energy moving or the release of something I had kept hidden. This discomfort frequently manifests in my bladder, lower back, and hips. Energy healers have said the same: "What is going on in your hips?" When I visit the doctor, they can't identify any cause, often suggesting arthritis.

Another perspective is that my body is merely trying to keep up with my spiritual growth. Growing pains, remember? After all, we are souls having a human experience. Because of this, I've learned to trust my own judgment regarding these symptoms and often ask Spirit for guidance.

These are just a few of my experiences during my spiritual awakening, and there are many more, including feelings of suddenly losing my identity, moments of fear, and the push to move forward. I began to engage in deep self-reflection, pondering my purpose and whether I'm on the right path. Even now this seems to be a recurring theme almost every day, especially if things are going my way, because I worry that I'm not following my inner guidance *enough*. Some of these thoughts are undoubtedly my ego mind trying to convince me that this is all nonsense, or they are vestiges from old patterns of self-doubt.

I'm not sharing all of this to scare you in any way; rather, I want to give you a glimpse of what it can sometimes feel like. We all process things differently, but I genuinely believe that if you are meant to go through a spiritual awakening, there's nothing that can prevent it. It is meant to be; you are evolving and simply trying your hardest to keep up.

Mine has had its ups and downs, but I always return to my trust in Spirit and the understanding that *I can ask for help with anything.* Your spiritual team is eager to assist you with issues great and small. I have spoken to many different Guides, some of my own and others who have come through readings of clients. These divine beings gently remind me what it is to be human. They have either lived lifetimes themselves or have guided countless souls through their earthly journeys and can relate to how hard it is to be a soul having a human experience. The wisdom and guidance they share reflects a deep understanding of our struggles, emotions, and pain. They deeply feel your emotions, whether you're happy or sad.

It takes courage to walk the path of your soul. I constantly remind myself to stand in my power, to embrace my experiences, and to live fully present in everyday moments because tomorrow is never guaranteed. A song that comes to mind is: "I Hope You Dance" by Lee Ann Womack.

Stand in your power and be an inspiration to others. Take ownership of your personal growth and the hard work you've put in to become who you are truly meant to be. You are resilient.

You, Beautiful Soul, are on a journey of self-discovery, making the connection between your inner self, the divine, and the world around you. This journey involves exploring your beliefs, understanding your emotions, and recognizing your unique gifts. As you navigate your path, you may encounter signposts or aha moments along the way that encourage growth and transformation. Embrace the process for it allows you to uncover deeper truths about who you are and what you're capable of. Trust that each step you take brings you closer to a more authentic and fulfilling life.

Remember, this journey is uniquely yours, and honoring your awakening is essential for personal growth and relationship with your soul.

You are the most important person in your life. Please take that to heart, as it's easy to lose ourselves in relationships, various situations, and life in general. And no matter what is happening around you, don't give up on yourself.

You matter, you are special, and you are loved.

CHAPTER NINE

Abundance of Gifts

When I began my spiritual awakening a few years ago, I had little understanding of what spiritual gifts were. I had been able to relay messages from loved ones who had passed away a few times, but honestly, I never saw myself as a medium. I still struggle with that label. The idea of identifying as a psychic or medium is an ongoing process unfolding for me, even though it is one of my gifts.

I occasionally used to watch the TV show *Long Island Medium* with Theresa Caputo. Many years before I discovered my own gifts and abilities, I was always moved by how she brought forth messages of healing and comfort to those longing for a connection. I thought it was so cool that she could do that, and I even bought a couple of her books.

Reading them changed my perspective, helping me realize

that our loved ones who have passed are at peace and that we are all connected in some way. It gave me a whole new outlook on life. She also shared stories about her grandmother, who would visit her as a big black fly, and one time landed on her cupcake just to grab her attention. This made me reflect on my nan, who I often sensed was near, appearing as a bird from time to time. Shortly after reading Caputo's first book, I felt a shift in perception. As I sat outside, a beautiful yellow bird landed near me. It stopped for just a brief moment, but it was enough to catch my attention, and I instantly knew it was my nan saying hello. This has happened more than once.

Over the course of two years, I discovered many gifts as I deepened my understanding of myself and my new direction in life. I decided to take a *Tarot* course, feeling a strong pull toward divination with cards. I found it fascinating that Tarot originated in the 1400s in Italy.

Who knew that these cards contained so many hidden meanings and that I could use them for guidance in my life and the lives of others? I felt a genuine calling for this. It took me about a year to fully understand their meanings and to trust my intuition and the guidance from Spirit in order to assist someone in making a decision or choosing a direction.

The more I read the cards, the more I learned to trust the messages they conveyed. I have attended several expos and provided readings, which I love doing, and I am continually amazed by how accurate they have been. Tarot is a wonderful tool for life guidance, and I pull a card daily for myself from the Rider-Waite Tarot. I use this deck a lot, and you can tell by how worn the edges are around the corners, but for me, this adds to the connection. I also love Kyle Gray's Decks. He is known as the

"Angel Whisperer." I have all his decks. I enjoy the messages they express. (See Resources in back for more about those and other Tarot decks I recommend.)

When I do Tarot readings for others, I always begin by asking if they have a question for the cards. Most often they do not. In those moments I rely on my intuition and let the cards guide the reading. It took time for me to truly trust myself and the messages coming through, but now I simply open, receive, and the insight flows. Even without a specific question, the reading will touch something deep within them, and then they begin to open up and share what's truly going on in their lives.

One example of a reading I did was for a woman in her late 40s who was thinking about starting her own herbal business. She had a knack for creating tinctures, candles and bath salts, but lacked the confidence to take the leap. The reading highlighted her natural skills, resources, and the potential for success—if she acted on her ideas. The advice was straightforward: Take a leap of faith. And that's exactly what she did. Later, she told me it was the best guidance she had received in years.

About a year after I started working with Tarot cards, I stumbled upon an article about *natal chart readings* and felt a strong desire to learn more. These are an interpretation of your birth chart, like a map of the sky at the exact moment and location of your birth. The chart includes positions of the Sun, Moon, Planets, and Astrological Houses, offering insights into personality traits, life patterns, strengths, potential paths and even karmic lessons. A natal chart reading can be a powerful tool for self-discovery, offering a comprehensive view of various dimensions of your life to help you navigate challenges, opportunities, and personal growth. Your natal chart can provide a deeper understanding of your spiritual inclinations and highlight areas where you may seek growth or development.

Some readings explore potential health-related predispositions linked to specific astrological placements. Additionally, certain astrologers may interpret aspects of your natal chart in the context of past lives, suggesting lessons or patterns that carry over into this lifetime. The chart can also pinpoint significant life events and periods of growth, change, or challenge. It is the best gift you can give yourself.

Ultimately, a natal chart offers insights into your life's purpose and the lessons you are meant to learn throughout your journey, which has been incredibly helpful for me.

My friend Ashley specializes in astrology readings, so I reached out to her. She is incredibly intuitive, and her insights have been profoundly helpful on my journey. When she read my natal chart, it clarified so much about my life path, revealing that I had been a healer in many past lives and had carried that ability into this lifetime.

And I learned that this gift was connected to my hands. I wondered what that meant. This idea came up again in another session, where it was suggested that I consider taking a *Reiki* class. I knew someone who taught Reiki classes, so she organized a weekend class for a few of us.

Reiki truly felt like my calling. I felt deeply connected to energy and could literally feel it in my hands. Not only that, but I could also see things about people and intuitively know things about them. I learned I possess the gift of seeing past lives, which is one of my strongest abilities. I can't express how amazing it is. I don't even need to lay hands on anyone; I see scenes from the past as if watching a vision unfold before me. These glimpses often come with vivid detail, locations, emotions, and even names. Sometimes I'm able to ask for more information like whether a soul from that lifetime is present again in this one, perhaps as a family member or a close connection.

After I passed the Reiki I and II courses, I followed this calling to help others. I started by reaching out to a friend who had suffered a back injury. Lori was my first client and was open to trying it. The insights that flowed in while I was clearing and removing energy from her body were astounding—life-changing for both of us. This was one of my first experiences of seeing a past life.

I had a vision of her as a small child drowning at night. Before telling her what I was seeing, I asked whether she had a fear of water or drowning.

She responded, "Yes, at night."

In that moment I knew that vision was of her past life. It was so surreal to witness it firsthand. I now utilize all of these gifts during what I refer to as Intuitive Healing Sessions These sacred soul-centered experiences, are moments where energy, insight, and Spirit come together in service of deep healing and remembrance. Through guided insight, I draw upon a variety of modalities such as Reiki healing, channeled messages, glimpses into past lives, energetic clearing and chakra alignment. Each healing is tailored to what your soul needs most in the moment. I always let Spirit lead, and no two sessions are the same.

During these sessions, the ringing in my right ear often will intensify as it acts as a direct line to Source, providing me with a wealth of information, ranging from insights what I learned to call the *Akashic Records,* a vast energetic archive of every soul's journey, thoughts, and actions across all lifetimes, information related to health, details about the client's spirit animals (also known as *totems*), Guides, Angels, and loved ones. With so much information pouring in, I often wondered if I would be able to remember it all. However, with Spirit's assistance, I did remember, and now, I make it a practice to record each session so my clients can revisit the messages, because often there's more to receive the second time around.

Another session stands out the most, perhaps because of the deep personal connection I had with the person involved. His name was Ron, and his wife, Dawn, is not only someone I had worked alongside but also one of my closest friends.

Dawn had been part of my spiritual awakening from the very beginning. She was surprisingly receptive to the changes in me, and I often shared my experiences with her. She supported me every step of the way as my gifts grew stronger.

Ron was an incredible man who would do anything for anyone. He was very well-known in our community and a very handsome cowboy, but most importantly a beautiful soul. He had been battling cancer for two years and was approaching the final chapter of his path on Earth. I asked if I could lay my hands on him, hoping to clear some energy and receive guidance from Spirit on how I could help.

When I arrived, I was struck by how much Ron had changed. He was thin, his once-strong frame now frail, the cancer having taken its toll. Yet, despite his condition, he never complained. Often, he even refused pain treatment.

I spent an hour clearing energy and using my gifts to ask Spirit about him. I could feel the heaviness of the cancer in certain areas, its weight lingering in the space around him. At that moment, I could see that Ron had once been a holy man, and I felt he had walked with Jesus. One of his Guides at the time was the Apostle Paul, and I had a vision of fish swimming all around him. His Guides and Angels informed me they were preparing him for his transition. Afterward Ron appeared calm and deeply at peace and showed heartfelt gratitude for the support.

I knew he was in good hands, and his suffering was almost over, yet my heart ached, knowing he would not be with us much longer. Even more painful was witnessing Dawn, my dear friend, as she watched the love of her life, her husband of twenty-nine years, slowly slip away. When Ron crossed over, he left behind a beautiful legacy. He was so much more than his illness; he was a devoted husband, father and grandfather, a Vietnam veteran—a man who lived with quiet strength, humility, and unwavering kindness. He never hesitated to help someone in need. His deep roots in the community were evident in his long-standing role with the Days of '76 Rodeo where he served on the board numerous times. His absence was deeply felt.

Ron visits from time to time, his presence a gentle unseen warmth that wraps around Dawn like a loving embrace. He lets her know she is deeply loved and never alone. His spirit lingers close, reminding her that their love for each other transcends the physical world. He is not truly gone, just beyond the veil, in another room of the divine home we all share. Their souls remain forever connected, bound by love that not even death can sever.

All of our loved ones are just a breath away. Their essence lingers in the spaces between moments, in the soft rustle of leaves, in the sun's tender touch on your cheek, in the call of a bird, in the flight of a butterfly, or in a familiar memory or song. You can call upon them at any time, and they will hear you. Their love is unconditional, eternal, and ever-present. They walk beside you, guiding, comforting, and surrounding you with their light. All you need to do is open your heart, and you will feel them near.

I have been deeply blessed to have many clients return for follow-up appointments. It is an honor to assist them on their journey, offering guidance, healing, and messages of hope and love. Being able to serve as a channel for Spirit and bring comfort fills my heart with gratitude.

Along my journey, I learned more about spirit animals and their connection to us. Each of us has one or more spirit animals, including a totem spirit animal who remains with us throughout our lives. The others may come and go, like our team of spiritual helpers, depending on where we are in our journey and what we need.

As for the Angels, I believe they have been with us since the moment of conception. I call my Guardian Angel Luculia. All Angels have names, but sometimes they offer a shortened version, knowing we could never pronounce their true name. Their beauty is magnificent. To feel the presence of an Archangel, such as Michael, Uriel, Raphael, or Gabriel, is pure grace. I see them not as male or female, simply as divine beings.

One question a client asked me was whether a miscarriage involves a soul, and I believe it does. I have received messages from babies who did not make it through the pregnancy, but their sweet little presence was still very real and important.

Having spiritual gifts from heaven is a sacred blessing, and embracing them can open the door to a deeply fulfilling journey, one that not only enriches your own soul but also brings light and healing to those around you. Your spiritual team may include: Angels, Spirit Guides, Animal Totems, and even higher-dimensional beings, such as Starseeds, including Lemurians, Pleiadeans, and Sirians, who, according to many spiritual teachings, are advanced souls from other solar systems who have incarnated on Earth to assist in its healing and ascension. Divine loving guidance surrounds us, offering wisdom, protection, and gentle reassurance that we are never truly alone.

In the chapters ahead, I will share more of my profound experiences with these divine beings and the ways they have touched my life.

If you want to learn more about anything I've mentioned, there is a wealth of content available to read or listen to. While much of it is fascinating, some of it might seem a bit far-fetched; however, after experiencing so many moments with Spirit, I now believe that anything and everything is possible. I will list some books, videos, websites in the Resources in the back of this book. Trust your intuition on which hold value for you. My path as an intuitive healer continues, and so does my desire to learn more.

An abundance of spiritual gifts exists within each of us, unique abilities waiting to be uncovered. I believe that divine timing plays a crucial part in our journeys; as we grow spiritually, our gifts unfold at their own pace. I encourage you to explore your own spiritual gifts and heed your intuition. Nothing in life will empower you more than this.

You are gifted, you are guided,
and your presence is a blessing.

CHAPTER TEN

Relationships and Forgiveness

As I began contemplating this book, I asked Spirit what I needed to include and even what I should name it. With each chapter, I have received guidance from my spiritual team, and what amazes me is that two years ago, a friend told me she sensed I would write a book, and that Archangel Chamuel would assist me. Of course, I thought, "Seriously?" I would have never dreamed it, yet here I am, and this book is now in your hands or on your screen. Today, I pulled the Chamuel card from my Angelic Activations Oracle deck by Kyle Gray. This confirmed that I'm on the right path in writing this book and chapter.

Forgiveness has emerged frequently during many of my readings and intuitive energy sessions. It has the ability to heal even the deepest wounds. I've found that, for me, forgiveness was not easy when it came to those who deeply hurt me, especially during my childhood.

Healing from past traumas begins with forgiving not just others but also yourself. Even if consciously, you believe the other person was the aggressor or in the wrong, some part of you may have been blaming yourself. For example, in my case I have sometimes wondered why I didn't tell anyone about my father's molestations. We have to stop blaming the victim. Yet in some cases, responsibility is more of a two-way street, such as in a marriage, friendship, or work relationship. Forgive yourself because you did the best you could with the level of knowledge and understanding you had at the time. Even if you think you made a mistake, you need to let go because holding onto anger, regret, and blame serves no beneficial purpose. They gnaw away at you, ultimately becoming a way of life. Anger has a way of surfacing at any given moment and can influence your relationships, making it essential to address these wounds in order to heal emotionally and spiritually.

There are plenty of books available on the topic, yet none of them resonated with me; in fact, they only intensified my anger. I had to dig deep to find the capacity to forgive others, but it was even more difficult to grant myself forgiveness.

Part of me argued: *Why do I need to forgive myself for something that was outside of my control? I didn't do anything wrong.*

Another part of me argued: *I was wrong, I've always been wrong one way or another, and I am unworthy of forgiveness.*

And yet a third, wiser, kinder voice whispered: *I can forgive myself, even if I don't know what (or whether) I've ever done anything wrong. Because this will set me free.*

Why are we so hard on ourselves for the wrongdoings of others? I've asked that question many times, and I believe it's largely because, as children, we are conditioned to perceive ourselves in relation to the actions of others. We often absorb the hurtful behaviors directed at us, leading us to feel responsible for the pain inflicted by others. This conditioning creates a pattern of self-blame and can make it hard for us to recognize our own worth and to appropriately hold others accountable for their actions.

This led me to direct my anger inward. As a result, I became difficult to be around at times. I felt miserable, and when a memory resurfaced or when someone spoke to me in a particular way, I would sink into a depressed state. For me, that felt like entering into darkness. I had been there so many times that it strangely felt safe and provided a sense of comfort.

However, I also felt that I wasn't alone in that darkness, and I always believed I would eventually find my way out and seek the light at the end of the tunnel. Sometimes I still feel the urge to retreat to that dark place, but I resist it, because I know I can't hide from the emotions I'm feeling. Instead, Spirit encourages us to ask ourselves why we are feeling this way and to take a moment to sit with those feelings rather than react to them.

Who do we need to forgive, and how do we forgive them?

This approach has been immensely helpful for me; by not reacting to the emotion and simply acknowledging it for what it is, I can keep it from taking control over me. Do I remember to do this all the time? No, sometimes I slip back into my old ways of thinking, but I know I have the spiritual guidance to turn it around.

Forgiveness didn't happen overnight; it is a process I work on every day. And it's not just about healing old wounds but also addressing new ones as they arise. It can feel at times like a never-ending cycle; just when you close one door of forgiveness, another one opens.

When I began my spiritual awakening, I also began the work of transformation. I started to see and feel things differently, and I worked diligently to release what no longer served me. Spirit encourages us to let go of anything that holds us back or hinders our spiritual growth, and that starts with forgiveness of others and self.

Spirit impressed upon my heart that the one person I truly needed to forgive was my ex-husband, and that I should reach out to him to seek his forgiveness. I grappled with this, and it took me some time to actually follow through. Although I knew deep down that it was essential for my continued healing, I still resisted the idea.

Eventually, I called Phillip and asked for his forgiveness for any pain I had caused during our marriage. In return, he asked for my forgiveness as well.

I was amazed by how sincere he sounded when he said it. To be honest, I wasn't sure he would respond, and I'm sure he wasn't expecting a call from me.

That call marked a pivotal shift in my journey by allowing me to release that part of me and our relationship which no longer served me or us. It was incredibly healing for both of us.

When it came to forgiveness of my parents, that took a little longer as I had repressed memories, especially when it came to my dad.

Here is another behavior from him that I am still working

on forgiving: My dad didn't show much interest in either of my children until my daughter turned five, and then suddenly, he wanted to have her for the weekend, but not my son. Remember: I was five when he began to sexually abuse me.

The kids had visited his home a few times for birthday parties but never stayed overnight. The thought of her spending the night there made me uncomfortable, and the image of him changing her into her nightgown or even putting her to bed made my skin crawl. More than a discomfort, it was a deeply unsettling unease, almost a revulsion, and I just could not grasp why, but I was unable to shake it. It also unsettled me that he didn't want my son to come.

My instinct chose in the end to say no.

Thank you, God, for protecting my daughter from what likely would have been a dangerous and devastating situation.

My dad became quite angry with my decision and expressed it very vocally, as if I were keeping his grandchildren away from him. I was actually trying to keep my daughter *safe* from him.

In his frustration, he even called Phillip to suggest that I wasn't mentally stable and might need help or even commitment! It was deeply disturbing to think that my dad wanted me committed simply because I wouldn't allow my daughter to spend the night with him. Part of me believed he realized that I was starting to remember events from my childhood, and he feared being exposed as a child molester, so he wanted me locked away and silenced.

The truth was that I had begun to remember, and it filled me with an awful feeling that he would somehow try to take her from me or traumatize her.

Thankfully, Phillip didn't believe a word my father said and dismissed his threats. We ultimately chose to move back to Belle Fourche, SD, as far away as we could from my dad. This meant pulling our daughter out of school halfway through the year, packing everything we could into our two vehicles, and leaving the rest and the past behind. It was the right choice.

After that, I hardly ever heard or spoke to my dad, and we never saw each other again.

At the time, I told myself I was OK with that. He scared me. I lived with the fear that one day he might show up and try to take my children. I even had dreams he was chasing me. No matter where I went, he found me.

Still, beneath the fear, there was always a small part of me that wondered how he was. The more spiritually awakened I became, the more I find myself pondering the "what ifs." What if things had been different? What if he had found healing too?

However, as more memories from my childhood began to resurface, they initiated an intense immersion into healing, including counseling to address the trauma I had repressed. This took time to process and work through, but my spiritual awakening has helped me understand that part of my soul's path in a different light.

To forgive him wasn't easy, but now, I am grateful to Spirit for every experience because it all led me to where I am today: helping others on their healing journeys.

A couple of years ago, I reached out. I wanted to do so in an indirect way, so I asked a friend in Texas if she would inquire whether my father would be interested in visiting with me.

His response? He "needed to consult his pastor to determine if it was a sign from God."

At first, I laughed. Doesn't God work through us? Then I

wondered if Spirit guided me or simply my human side longed to reconnect, especially since I felt there was so much left unsaid. I genuinely wanted to know how he was doing and had long since forgiven him.

I never learned what his pastor's advice was. He ignored me completely. A year later, he passed away from a heart aneurysm, dying alone. Melanie had been hospitalized with multiple sclerosis at the time of his death. I never had the chance to say goodbye, and perhaps that was exactly how it was meant to be. I believe Spirit stepped in, and this soul connection no longer served me.

I attended his funeral in Humble, Texas, which provided an opportunity to reconnect with some individuals from the church I had attended many years earlier. I also saw Melanie and got to meet one of my nephews, Joe, whom I knew nothing about, a son of my half-brother, Jim, whom I had met on my second trip to Texas. Joe was only fifteen, and he seemed like a kind young man. Tall with long wavy hair, he carried quiet sadness in his eyes. I could feel the heartbreak he was holding over the loss of his grandad. He attended the funeral alongside his mother, and my stepmom. It was such a shock to meet this nephew, and also to find out that apparently, I had *many* nieces and nephews.

People told me that Jim was largely absent from his own son's life. How sad! The old saying came to mind: "Like father like son."

My half-brother, Jim, was not present at our father's funeral. Jim did reach out to me by phone after the funeral, presumably because he had heard there might be a will. I had not been aware of one but said I would investigate it. During our conversation, he mentioned that his younger sister (no connection to me) had been abused and raped by our dad at age eight. I'm not certain how long that went on for. Apparently, the rape had been reported by Jim's mom and later gone to court but was dropped due to lack of evidence. My heart broke for his younger sister and the deep trauma she must carry now. I could understand then why he didn't attend the funeral. At the same time, I felt a strange sense of validation, proof that he had done this to other girls and that I was not alone.

It became clear that there was no inheritance, and everything had been left to Melanie and her family, nothing left to us, his own children. I let Jim know then never heard from him again. I heard he is working somewhere in Texas, on an oil field.

At the funeral, I was shocked to see that Melanie was in a wheelchair. She had been quite ill from MS and had spent some time in a nursing facility. During our conversation, she assured me that she had played no part in my dad's decision not to reconnect with me. Part of me wanted me to believe her, but another still sensed that she may have influenced his choice. She also thanked me for attending. That was the last contact we had. She passed away a year after my dad's passing.

I later learned that her mother had moved into their home and removed all items that belonged to my dad. Thankfully, I have a couple of photos of him when he was young, a couple of us from my first visit, and a handful of him with my children. I have none of us together when I was little. I believe my mum removed all traces of him. The pictures I have are just small snapshots in time, but they are all I have left to remind me that—for a brief moment—we tried to find our way back to one another.

My dad had been gone for just over a year when I first heard from him—from the other side. I had booked a session with Psychic Medium Dani Jo, primarily to learn how she tuned in and what I could gain from the experience. During that session, both my grandparents came through, as well as my dad, which surprised me as he was not the one I had hoped to hear from. Nevertheless, he made his presence known and expressed compassion and sadness for everything I had to endure. Years ago, I had let go of any hatred or anger toward him, allowing me to receive his message with an open heart. He acknowledged that there were many things left unsaid but ultimately conveyed that he was doing well. As a soul, he had chosen those lessons for his spiritual growth, which, in turn, contributed to mine as well.

My mum passed away in October 2025, shortly before the publication of this book. I'm so grateful that we had forgiven each other. I needed to forgive her for the cruelty I experienced growing up, and she needed to forgive me for leaving her to go live with my dad and settling in the United States. I can see now why she felt abandoned, even though that was not my intention. Over the many years since I moved here, I frequently would go back to the UK to visit her and my stepdad. We shared profound moments that brought us closer than ever. I truly believe that Spirit played a significant role in this, showing me that *healing is possible in any relationship—as long as both people want to heal.*

I also learned that even when someone isn't able to meet us in that healing, we can still connect with their Higher Self. Through prayer, intention, and visualization, we can ask for healing on a soul level, for their highest good and our own. This kind of spiritual forgiveness creates freedom. It allows us to release the pain of the past and make space for peace in the present and possibly in the future.

I once read a quote from author David Dayan Fisher: "The greatest gift of your life is your parents' dysfunction. Being aware of it, having forgiveness and compassion for it, gaining a greater understanding because of it, and healing from it—that is the true gift you have been given."

I love both my mum and dad with all my heart. I believe that one day I will reunite with them as souls. They are part of my soul family, and I have no doubt that we will come together in future lifetimes, playing different roles.

But even though I have forgiven, it doesn't mean I will ever forget. I've simply chosen not to dwell on it anymore, focusing instead on what is in front of me rather than what is behind me. I can honestly say that not much emotion arises as I write this chapter, which proves that I have done the self-work necessary for healing, releasing, and forgiving along with the work on releasing self-judgment. I also learned to be compassionate toward myself, which is vital for genuine healing.

Self-acceptance and forgiveness are not just acts of kindness toward others, but also sacred gifts you give yourself. As you navigate your own journey, remember that healing takes time, and it's OK to seek help and express your feelings. I am grateful for the insights from the angelic realm and the wonderful souls who have stood by my side in the process. Forgiveness is our friend and not our enemy.

Forgiveness is a sacred gift you give to yourself as well as others.

CHAPTER ELEVEN

Angels, Guides, and Energies Felt but Unseen

This is one of my favorite subjects, which I have briefly referred to in other chapters. The fact that these spiritual beings exist and that there is so much more divine wisdom available to us is not only amazing but also comforting, reminding us that we are not alone.

I personally have two Angels and seven Guides. I know the names of my Angels and almost all of my Guides. I've been told that Joan of Arc is one of my Guides, along with Edgar Cayce. I often hear the quote, "I am not afraid. I was born to do this," attributed to Joan of Arc. If you'd like to ask for your Guides' names, you can. Listen closely, and you will hear them. Be patient as it sometimes doesn't happen in that moment—but keep asking. If you want confirmation, request to see or hear the name elsewhere. For example, their name may be mentioned in a conversation, or you may be guided through a synchronicity, to a certain article, book, song, or website.

How do you know when one of your Spirit Guides is with you? Whenever I sense a presence, I get a tingling sensation, or chills, and I can sense a subtle energy shift in the atmosphere. I always say, "We are not alone." In the beginning, I would say it out loud, because it filled me with awe and excitement, to truly know they are there in that exact moment. Sometimes my blurting this out would even make people jump or spill their coffee! I have toned it down some, but the thrill is still there. My friend Jackie expects me to say that at least once when we're together, then she giggles.

Recently, Tracy bought me a hat that says: "We are not alone." She laughed out loud when she found it, and her colleagues wondered what was so funny. She told them, "You have no idea," and she couldn't wait to give it to me. This made all of us laugh, especially Jackie.

I love that I have this ability, and I often get emotional as I feel honored to be in their presence. Being in the presence of an Angelic Being is an incredibly uplifting and calming experience. Angels' energy is of a higher vibration; it feels more intense along with a comforting warmth that may fill your entire being, making you feel safe and protected.

Everyone has at least one Angel and several Guides present in their lives simultaneously. The Angel has been with you since you arrived on Earth, while the Guides may come and go based on where you are in your journey. These Guides can be anyone who has lived as a human, including a loved one who has crossed over.

Or they could be an Ancestor, an Ascended Master, or even a Dragon. Yes, Dragons do exist in the spirit world. I have a Dragon who represents my Shadow Self; he is red and calls himself Raguel. I'm currently looking for the perfect tattoo that represents how I picture him.

Now let's talk about Shadow Work. What is it? And what is your Shadow Self?

Here is a brief description: Shadow Work is a spiritual practice focused on exploring and integrating the unconscious aspects of ourselves, commonly referred to as the "Shadow." These are parts of our personality that we may suppress, deny, or ignore because they are seen as unacceptable or undesirable. The concept of the Shadow comes from the work of Carl Jung, who believed that embracing and understanding these hidden aspects can lead to greater self-awareness and personal growth.

"Until you make the unconscious conscious,
it will direct your life,
and you will call it fate."
— Carl Jung

During a Shadow Work retreat hosted by Dani Jo, we engaged in a meditation that encouraged us to seek out our Shadow Selves. I didn't understand what that meant but chose to trust the process. I could hear others expressing excitement as they discovered theirs; some saw their Shadow Self as a tree or an animal. But as hard as I tried, I couldn't find or visualize mine.

Then I sensed a path ahead and felt a warm energy, noticing an orange glow in the distance. Others were sharing about their visualizations and perceptions, and I shared that I felt frustrated.

Our host asked everyone to meditate on my behalf to help me make the connection.

It wasn't long before I felt my Shadow Self, and that's when the excitement began. The house started to make noises! Everyone could hear glasses clinking upstairs. Then the refrigerator began producing some very strange sounds: a loud banging coming from the door as if something was trying to escape, and the sound of glass breaking coming from inside it.

Then suddenly, the fire in the fireplace went out!

I sat up and exclaimed, "He's here!"

Dani Jo asked, "Who's here?"

I replied, "My Dragon!"

Later, she jokingly told me that at the time she thought she might need to perform an exorcism.

At that moment, I became known as "the lady with the red fire Dragon."

Psychic Medium Dani Jo's compassionate guidance created a space for deep healing and transformation, allowing participants to safely explore the parts of themselves that's often kept hidden. Shadow work can be emotional, as buried aspects of the self-rise to the surface, but Spirit encourages us to meet those parts with unconditional love. If you are feeling called to this kind of soul-centered work, I encourage you seek out a trusted practitioner in your area who can hold that space with care and integrity. One might assume that all Spirit Guides are human, or that all Animal Totems are simply animals, but that's not always the case. In my experience, I've brought through several powerful Dragons, each a different color and with a unique energy. Some of these Dragons appear as Spirit Guides or Elementals (more on those later) and others come through as Animal Totems, showing that the spiritual realm is much more diverse and nuanced than we may expect.

Let me tell you about a dream Albert had a few years ago. He dreamed we were at our hunting camp in Lemmon, South Dakota when a small plane (probably a crop duster) landed in the field nearby. I am not a hunter myself, but Albert has always loved it.

A man exited the plane, then asked, "What do you think of my plane?"

Albert responded, "That's great, but check *this* out!"

Then I appeared—sitting on my red Dragon!

Albert never mentioned its name but because he was red, I assumed it was Raguel. It makes me smile every time I think about it.

Now let's talk about our Ancestors. They could be from hundreds or even thousands of years in the past. I have encountered a few Medicine Men and Women, and they are incredibly powerful and protective of the souls they're with. In fact, a client's Ancestors sometimes visit me before I begin a session to let me know they are watching. I reassure them that their descendants are in good hands.

Dragons are Spirit Animals of a more mythological (yet spiritually real) sort, and there are many other types of Spirit Animals, all a delight. They can be pets that have crossed over. I have brought through many pets; they, too, want their human to know they are safe. This brings a lot of comfort. My Sunny has visited me in dreams many times.

Everyone has a main Totem Spirit Animal, the one that has been with them from the very beginning. Mine is a Cat. Interestingly, I'm not particularly fond of Cats; they often make me feel like I have a hairball stuck in my throat. Yet mine is indeed a Cat, and they appear in my life unexpectedly, and frequent my dreams.

A Spirit Animal can be anything, such as a Bear, an Eagle, or even a Wolf. When I ask others if they would like to know their Spirit Animal, or Animals, this is because we can have several. People often hope for a Bear or some other large wild mammal. When I tell them it's a Grasshopper or a Bee, they look at me with disappointment. Yes, it can be an Ant, a Butterfly, a Flamingo, or even a Giraffe! Each one represents something unique, with its own meaning and purpose. They can also come and go, much like our Guides. At the moment, one of mine is a Skunk.

There are many books that provide various interpretations of Spirit Animals and what they symbolize for you. I will include a list of my favorites at the end of this book.

Now let's explore Light Beings. While Angels, Guides, and Spirit Animals are considered Spiritual Beings, when I say Light Beings, I am referring specifically to those thought to exist in dimensions beyond normal space and time. These entities are sometimes referred to as Starseeds or even Alien life forms. I always have felt that we are not alone in more ways than one; after all, why would God create just one world full of life when He created so many life forms right here on Earth, such as animals, insects, trees, and even us?

Humanity will become aware of more Starseeds in the near future. I have encountered several Light Beings during my sessions and have channeled a few different ones.

One time, during a hypnosis session, I began to channel a group that identified themselves as the "I Am Jesuit." While channeling them, I spoke in a different manner and conveyed messages about their race and our planet as a whole. They also conveyed how we are all connected through consciousness and that Earth is merely a speck in the grand scheme of things. This message came through in their language:

Ikíhife hinei rákewa anei ráki inei rá'onei,
imei rá kóhaka kénei, ajinei ráku'ono.
Translation:
"We rise together in the breath of the dawn.
Each moment is a sacred seed of change,
Planted in the heart of all that is becoming."

The "I Am Jesuit" are from the Orion Nebula. I feel a connection to that place with my soul. How do you feel when you read these words, in either form?

I also have a female Light Being who identifies as Sensi; *sensei* means "teacher" in Japanese. Sensi has been assisting a group of us in writing a book on the vortexes or energy centers in the Black Hills, such as Devils Tower located in Wyoming. The group includes Ashley, Jackie, Tracy, and myself. Together we have been exploring these sacred sites, each bringing our own intuitive insights and spiritual gifts to the project. Additionally, Sensi mentioned that in the near future, we will be called upon collectively to use these vortexes to help heal the planet. Then I felt her words come through in a poem:

Rise from the ashes, feet in the sand.
Move with grace, you are one with the land.

So, what does that mean for us? Let's start with Collective

Consciousness; we are all interconnected, and our individual and collective actions can influence the well-being of the Earth and its inhabitants. We have a sense of unity and shared purpose.

These Light Beings often serve as catalysts for awakening more people to their spiritual gifts and responsibilities. The involvement of Light Beings like Sensi can remind us that we have support from higher realms in our efforts to create positive change, reinforcing the idea that we are not alone in our endeavors. (There, I said it again!)

What about energies that don't feel light and appear darker? I have experienced such things in the middle of the night and even in the middle of the day. I have encountered spirits, some of whom may be referred to as ghosts, who are looking to pass through or even need a little help crossing over.

People often ask me: "Why are ghosts still here? Why didn't they follow the Light?"

That is a good question, and I have asked the same. The best answer that resonated with me was from Edgar Cayce, who believed that some souls might remain in the earthly realm due to unfinished business, emotional attachments, fear of judgment, or a desire to help loved ones. Occasionally, spirits may remain with the intention of assisting family members or friends, guiding them during difficult times. Cayce also emphasized the importance of guiding these souls toward the Light, suggesting that spiritual practices and prayers can help them find peace and complete their journeys.

I have helped several to cross over. For example, while I was sitting drinking a cup of tea, a man who called himself George spoke to me. He said he was just passing through and was looking for the exit.

I asked him gently, "Do you mean the way home?"

He said, "Yes! I am searching for my family, and for the Light. Can you help me?"

I called in guidance from Spirit to assist him in crossing over.

A few moments later, I could feel a shift in his energy as he began to let go. Calmness and peace filled the space. It was a beautiful sacred transition.

Sometimes I've had some unpleasant encounters. In such cases, energetically I feel I am not alone, but the energy doesn't feel comfortable. More creepy, darker, or even scary.

I have heard others speak of such energy as if it's something we ourselves created. "Face your own demons." Or: "Fear is an illusion. A projection."

I have pondered this a lot and feel that, yes, that could be a possibility depending on the situation or circumstance. But when our energy dips low, for example, through an addiction, like alcoholism and drug abuse, we can unknowingly open the doors to darker energies. In those moments, what we consume to escape can become an invitation for something far heavier to step in.

Maybe you yourself have crossed paths with such energy, those unsettling darker presences that can sometimes creep in through our dreams. Personally, I have felt them in my sleep, disturbing, shadowy figures that left me rattled upon waking. I've encountered those terrifying moments when I felt I couldn't move, as if something was holding me down, paralyzed and helpless. In those moments I could hear someone whispering, "Wake up.... It's time to wake up now." Was that Spirit or was it a deeper part of myself calling me back?

I've often found myself lucid in these dreams, fully aware,

yet unable to stop what's happening, as I'm watching it all unfold and unable to do anything to stop it. I couldn't change what was happening and yet through it all, I knew I wasn't alone. I would call on Archangel Michael and recite his prayer, burn sage, and ask Spirit to send the energy back from where it came, with love and light. Everything, even the darkest forces, comes from Source.

These events have only deepened my understanding of energy and the unseen realms and my faith in the divine protection that always surrounds us. It's important to remember that regardless of whether the energy is considered dark or light, all energy originates from the same source. Everything starts somewhere, everything eventually returns to that source, and we as souls are always protected.

But that does not mean harm never happens, because even though on the spiritual level we are infinite and untouched, on the human level and Earth plane, we can be affected. I do believe it is possible for darker energies to influence, attach, or manipulate, especially if one's energy is weakened and seeks to escape.

This is why *spiritual hygiene* matters. Awareness matters. Tending to your energy field matters. You are not crazy, and you are not imagining things! When left unaddressed, this kind of energetic interference can even manifest physically, through illness, fatigue, injuries, accidents, or unexplained symptoms, because the spiritual body and the physical body are always in conversation.

We all have the ability to pick up energy that doesn't belong to us. I have cleared various energies from clients who were unaware they had any attachments, yet they sensed that something felt off, like behaving in such a way they appear not to be themselves. Perhaps they felt heaviness, extra tired and a feeling being drained. Or they were dropping, losing, or bumping into things, having accidents, nightmares, or a run of "bad luck."

If this happens to you, remember to stay grounded, to clear your energy, and try not to bring anything home. Here are a few suggestions that can offer purification and relief, both spiritually and practically. I use these myself as part of my own energetic hygiene and protection.

Techniques for Spiritual Protection and Purification:

- Salt Baths (sea or Epsom salt) help draw out stagnant or unwanted energy. These days you can also buy Epsom salt in bubble bath form. You can add essential oils, like frankincense or even clove. Rose oil is good too. Even just water is amazing at washing away energy.

- Smudging or cleansing your space with sage or palo santo, can reset energy. If you can pick wild prairie sage, it's even better. I will tie it in bundles to dry hanging upside down on my porch. I'm fortunate to live in an area where sage grows freely.

- Sound carries intention. Tools like Tibetan singing bowls, chimes, bells, and tuning forks help to shift energy. These vibrations tend to clear stagnation, calm the nervous system and bring the body back into alignment. Each sound creates a vibration that awakens our natural balance and our connection to the Divine. I personally found chanting to be especially healing. I love to hum or chant quietly while in the bathtub; there's something soothing about combining water with vibration. My voice removes what I no longer need, make space for peace.

- Crystals like black tourmaline, obsidian, or selenite offer both protection and cleansing. I wear a bracelet with black tourmaline and hematite every day, even while I sleep, for energetic safety and grounding.

- Energetic cord cutting is a great tool. Visualize or call in Archangel Michael to assist with severing connections that are not serving your highest good. He carries a mighty sword for a reason! You can find many of his protection prayers online; they are simple, powerful, and easy to recite.

- Daily grounding (a.k.a. earthing) is a simple, effective way to clear unwanted energy. Walk barefoot on the earth, breathe deeply, and visualize roots extending from your feet into the land, going down beneath the surface, like a tree's roots. I live in an area where it's not always possible to physically connect to the earth during the winter, so instead, I visualize my roots stretching deep into the ground, sometimes even wrapping around the base of a tree. I have heard of others who live in urban areas keeping a pot or tray of dirt inside, so they can stand in it with their bare feet. It's a creative way to reconnect to the earth, especially when nature isn't accessible. You may also rub essential oils into the soles of your feet. Choose oils that feel grounding to you, such as pine, frankincense, vetiver, cedar, and patchouli. Maybe a grounding essential oil blend.

Know that you have the power to balance and clear energy. Trust in yourself.

There is a great deal we can, and should, do for ourselves and our energy, both for protection and for cleansing.

But sometimes we need further assistance, especially for issues or energies that are very heavy, old, or troublesome, or if we feel overwhelmed, weak, or like our tools just aren't working very well. If you feel drawn to get support with healing, or to seek guidance, practitioners like Reiki Masters, Shamanic Healers, and other Energy Healers specialize in clearing and balancing energy.

It is not a sign of weakness to get support. It is a sign of self-love.

Even healers need healing sometimes.

Finally, another type of Spiritual Being is an Elemental, which represents the forces of nature. These enchanting figures embody the magic and mystery of the natural world, captivating our imagination and inspiring countless tales and legends. Yes, I'm referring to Fairies, Gnomes, Leprechauns, Mermaids, Dyads, and other beings found in various spiritual and mystical traditions, including folklore. I have heard people talk about Elementals showing up during past-life regression sessions—fascinating to say the least.

Once, I asked if I could see an Elemental, and shortly after, a black butterfly landed right in front of me. Seeking confirmation, I wanted to ensure I was genuinely witnessing an Elemental. Later that day, while Albert and I were walking our dogs along a path in the woods, the same black butterfly landed in front of me again. It seems that butterflies can be considered Elementals. Or perhaps Fairies can take the form of butterflies.

Elementals are also associated with the four elements: Earth,

Air, Fire, and Water. We, too, are made up of all four elements. I identify mostly with Water, which explains my softness and adaptability, but I also carry a significant amount of Fire, which encourages me to seek out fun. I discovered all of this through my natal chart.

In summary, Angels, Guides, Spirit Animals, Ancestors, Elementals and more are all here to assist you on your spiritual journey and life path. I refer to your collection of all your Guides as your spiritual team. They are eager to help, and all you have to do is ask, and you shall receive.

Trusting in your intuition and having faith in your spiritual team can help you navigate challenges and foster personal transformation. I like to believe that we are stewards of the Earth, encouraged to tap into our gifts and the spiritual guidance available to us.

So, the next time you're walking in the woods, don't be surprised if a Fairy darts past your ear and offers a little greeting.

You are surrounded, you are protected,
and you are cherished.

CHAPTER TWELVE

Past Lives and Soul Connections

One of my strongest spiritual gifts is the ability to see others' past lives, including the individuals in their present lives who played significant roles in those previous existences. I have personally glimpsed a few of my own past lives and noticed that most of them carry a common theme, possibly because my soul didn't receive what it needed the first time around.

Many spiritual traditions suggest that unresolved issues or lessons from past lives can resurface in multiple lifetimes, including our current life, as karmic lessons, providing us with opportunities for healing and growth.

What's remarkable is that the people in our lives today—be

they romantic soulmates, friends, or family—often have held different roles in our past lives. In my own past lives, I held many positions as a religious leader, dating back as early as Atlantis. I also learned that I was Marcaria, the daughter of Hades and Persephone. I also have heard that Marcaria's true father was Zeus, who disguised himself as Hades to lie with Persephone. It's all quite fascinating, as the details about her lineage can vary depending on the sources of information you come across.

One common version of the legend says that Marcaria felt it was her responsibility or calling to watch over the souls of Atlantis. She stood up against her father, Hades, refusing to let him take them. Macaria is considered a goddess who presides over a blessed afterlife, to help humans have a peaceful existence after death. The name itself derives from the Greek word "makarios," which means "blessed" or "happy."

I remember communicating with Hades while holding a trident, a three-pronged spear, in my right hand. As Hades approached, I slammed it to the ground, and a wave of energy pushed him back. It felt like a very powerful moment. I also had a sister named Melinoë, who is now my friend Tracy.

I have experienced several past lives as a monk, including one in Switzerland, and one in Battle, England. I experienced both sides of the spectrum; at times, I inflicted abuse, while at other times I was abused within the walls of a church.

This past year, I felt an overwhelming urge to visit Battle after having dreamt about it. I spent a few days there exploring the abbey, and I sensed that my visit was a form of healing. My struggles with old habits and religious beliefs, which I believe I carried forward from those lifetimes, have made it tough to separate the present from the past.

Aligning myself with the present is an ongoing lesson, but I feel I have made significant progress. Many of my clients who are going through spiritual awakenings also have been monks in past lives. I often wonder if there is a connection in some way.

I had a past life as a fisherman in Jerusalem before the arrival of Jesus. I also was the wife of a Roman soldier who had an affair with my personal servant, who later became pregnant with my husband's child. Since I was unable to have children, this was an overwhelming insult and very hurtful to me. In my anger, I threw her into the mud in the street, where she was forced into prostitution and later took her own life. The slave is now my friend Tracy. Again!

In another life, I was a Roman slave assigned to Julius Caesar's lover. He had many lovers, but this particular one he was very affectionate toward. I was constantly nearby, attending to her every need and often present during their private moments. I wasn't supposed to be seen or heard, yet I was always there. Over time, I sensed he didn't trust my presence, as if he suspected I was listening, watching, and perhaps reporting on what I heard, spying. In truth, I wasn't a spy at all, though he clearly believed otherwise. He plotted to kill me by poisoning a drink. Fortunately, a Roman guard, whom I believe had a romantic relationship with, saved me by preventing me from drinking it. This Roman guard is now a close friend and the owner of a company that provided security for most of the events I coordinated. In that life, I did later die from poisoning, and I eventually learned that I had been his daughter in that lifetime, a child he himself never knew existed.

Sometimes we incarnate again very quickly, and other times we may take decades or centuries to do so, because our souls are waiting for just the right set of circumstances, soul family members in certain roles, even cultural and political situations, so we can learn what we need to learn and evolve into greater wisdom and kindness along the way.

I lived several lives in Egypt, where I was involved with the pyramids and their design. Psychic Medium Dani Jo once told me during an energy clearing that I still carry the pyramidal blueprints within my energy field around my hip area. This is particularly intriguing because I have been experiencing inexplicable problems with my hips, especially my left hip. I struggled to wrap my head around this concept (blueprints? in my hips?), but at this point, honestly, nothing would surprise me; there is so much we have yet to understand about our souls. I have seen a lot of clients with past lives in Egypt; many helped build the pyramids. Keep in mind that this makes sense because back in Egypt's golden age, many more thousands of people worked as slaves, compared to the ruling and merchant classes.

Some of my other past lives featured a recurring theme of suicide. I mentioned earlier in the book how I struggled with suicidal thoughts, and now I know the reasons behind them.

During a regression session with Tracy, I went back to the time of the Black Plague. I remember standing barefoot in the mud, overwhelmed by the stench of death in the air. I was a woman, a healer of some sort. With long black hair and torn clothing, I may have been viewed as a witch. I noticed a church in the distance with a tall steeple. There were soldiers everywhere, and I felt they were there to prevent anyone from leaving, as if the town were condemned to perish.

I felt profound grief from losing my children to the plague. With a knife in my right hand, I took my own life by slitting my throat. I remember dying, and then I saw a bright light before me.

A man approached, floating across the space, extending his hand and saying, "Child, you are forgiven." It was Jesus.

During that session, when I viewed the moment of slitting my throat, I began to choke and struggled to breathe, as if reliving the entire experience. It was a profound moment, and Tracy was a witness to it and offered support. She didn't just observe; as an empath, she experienced it with me.

I have a friend who was also part of that same past life. She was a man driving a cart to collect the dead. I remember hearing her call out: "Bring out your dead."

But, as far as I remember at this point, the very first time I took my own life was in a life when I knew Jesus. I remember visiting Mount Zion, standing in front of Jesus, and kissing him on the cheek.

Jesus said to me, "All is forgiven. You have served your purpose." I later hung myself.

Was I the man who betrayed Jesus, one of his disciples? It's difficult for me to even mention his name now. That past life is a heavy burden to bear, and I have spent a lot of time grieving and discussing it with my higher self. Spirit reassures me that it was part of the plan, and that I chose to embody that role in that lifetime. Nonetheless, no one wants to live with the idea of being the one who set in motion the events leading to Jesus' crucifixion.

But perhaps that sacrifice was necessary, not as an end but a doorway to something greater. His death was not a defeat, but a transformation. Through his resurrection, Jesus showed us that our souls are eternal, and that love transcends time.

"I am the light of the world.
Whoever follows me will not walk in darkness
but will have the light of life."
—John 8:12

And so, I have come to see Judas differently. Perhaps he was not cursed but chosen. Perhaps his role was not betrayal but sacrifice. A soul willing to carry the weight of history so that humanity could awaken to something greater. If that lifetime was mine, then I carry both the wound and the lesson: That even through darkness, light is born. That despair can be transformed into hope.

Jesus or Yeshua as I call him, did not see Judas as an enemy. He saw him as a brother. He knew the choice had been made long before either of them walked the Earth. And maybe that is the deeper truth, that each of us in different lifetimes are asked to play roles both heavy and light. Some bring comfort, others bring burdens. All necessary for the greater good. I wonder if my painful grappling with suicidal thoughts is something I need to overcome in this lifetime? Or are they echoes of long ago finally fading and asking to be acknowledged and released? I may not know the full answer yet, but I do know this: I will continue to trust my Higher Self and the guidance my soul offers, knowing it always leads me toward healing, truth, and light.

I have come to know two others who were disciples of Jesus. During a past-life regression, one of my clients, whom I believe was the Apostle Peter, regressed into vivid memories of that lifetime. As I listened, she described standing amongst a group of men, each one waiting to be baptized by Jesus. Overcome with emotion in that moment, I listened with my heart wide open. She spoke of standing in the doorway of the tomb where Jesus was laid to rest. Her vivid details described how she felt and the beautiful light that filled the tomb.

For a moment, I felt as if I too were standing right there with her. In that deeply spiritual space, an unexpected message came through my client for me. As I listened, I heard her mention the Lion of Judah, and I sensed there was a connection somehow. The Lion of Judah, mentioned in the Bible, is a powerful symbol of strength, courage, and divine leadership. It originates from the tribe of Judah, descended from King David and later Jesus.

"You are a lion's cub, Judah;
you return from the prey, my son.
Like a lion he crouches and lies downlike a lioness—
who dares to rouse him?
The scepter will not depart from Judah,
nor the ruler's staff from between his feet,
until he to whom it belongs- shall come
and the obedience of the nations shall be his."
— Genesis 49: 9-10

As I sat with this message, I asked Jesus: "What does this mean for me?" The sense I got was that it was a divine affirmation, a reminder that I carry spiritual strength, courage, and divine purpose.

There are indeed connections between the issues we face in our current lives and the past lives we shared with those around us in this life. My now husband, Albert, and I lived together in a past life in Germany during World War II, in a small apartment. I vividly remember hearing planes flying overhead in the darkness. I stood on the balcony and looked down at the street below, where people had gathered, all looking up in fear. As I met their gazes, I didn't see them as ordinary faces; I sensed them as souls, many of whom felt as though they had already crossed over, perhaps victims of the war itself. Their presence carried a weight of sorrow and remembrance, as if they were showing themselves to be seen and acknowledged. As we were lying on the floor holding each other as bombs began to fall, I could feel his heart racing. Eventually, we moved to the bathroom with our two dogs, whom we knew in this life as Koko and Sunny. Yes, even our pets have been part of our past lives. I'm not sure if we died during that time, but if we did, I'm sure we crossed over together.

This concept of past lives emphasizes that growth is a continuous journey, where each lifetime provides lessons that contribute to the evolution of our soul. Unresolved issues or lessons from past lives can reappear in our current life as karmic lessons, offering us opportunities for healing and growth. Past lives may help us find a pathway to healing deep-seated wounds, as we learn to address and resolve the root causes of our own struggles.

Overall, the idea of past lives and recurring themes invites a reflective exploration of our life, helping us gain understanding and insight into our experiences. I encourage you to explore your past lives, whether through a Past-Life Regression session (in which you and/or the hypnotherapist or intuitive may view, hear, or just know information about your past lives), by consulting a Psychic Medium (who can clairaudiently hear or clairvoyantly see your past lives, then relay that to you), or simply by asking your Higher Self for guidance.

I haven't mentioned Twin Flames until now, but I will touch on the subject briefly, as Spirit has indicated that I will be writing a separate book about this soon. The concept of having a twin soul is often described as two halves of the same soul, or mirror souls, signifying a deep, intense connection between two individuals. There is truth in this idea, and I see it as One Soul, Two Flames. Synchronicities, intense chemistry, and feelings of being "home" when with the other person are all very real.

I have yet to meet anyone who has encountered their Twin Flame and said, "That was amazing, let's do it again!" The experience is often intense, transformative, and far from easy. If you want a visual representation of how a Twin Flame connection can feel, I highly recommend watching the movie *Hancock* as it captures the powerful, chaotic, and deeply magnetic nature of this kind of bond.

Most people are no longer in contact with their Twin Flame. I believe that we encounter them in every life. That holds true for my twin and me. I crossed paths with mine two years ago, but we had known each other for seventeen years. The whole Twin Flame connection can be truly beautiful, yet it can be gut-wrenching at times. Several clients have shared their own Twin Flame encounters with me, each one unique. Some were romantically involved, while others felt a deep inexplicable connection, not realizing it might be a Twin Flame bond. Often their stories ended in separation, not always dramatic, sometimes it faded or quietly unraveled. Yet no matter the outcome, the truth remains: Twin Flames are never truly apart. That cord of soul connection doesn't break, even when life takes them in separate directions. And once they find each other, their lives are forever changed.

I've also been asked: "Is it possible to have two Twin Flames?" No I don't believe you can.

Also: "Are all Twin Flame connections romantic?" No, I don't think they are. But the feeling, the recognition, can still be there.

It's much more complex than most people think. However, there is no doubt that when you meet your Twin Flame, you will recognize them, as the energy between you is undeniably connected, you both will feel that bond—and that never goes away. Your Twin Flame can be significantly younger or older than you; they don't have to be the same age or race. It's as if you both chose to enter this life at different times and decided to cross paths at a particular moment in your journey.

The primary purpose of a Twin Flame connection is to teach you to love yourself.

Loving your twin unconditionally equates to loving yourself unconditionally.

This connection can trigger a lot within you.

I had known Brian for nearly seventeen years. A biker, who would come to town each summer for Sturgis Motorcycle Rally, a big event held the beginning of August. He would spend almost two weeks in Deadwood, meeting up with old friends in the evening Brian would spend the day riding with his biker buddies and then gamble at night. I would always see him sitting on a bench outside the hotel, drinking a cup of coffee. From the New York area, he had a noticeable accent. A few tattoos and a ring on every finger. Tall and built. I jokingly asked him if he were a gangster. He'd just smile and laugh but never really gave me an answer. He had been a Vietnam Vet, then a steel worker, now retired. He loved to fix cars or motorcycles.

In the beginning our conversations were light, simply hello and small talk about the Rally, but over the years they grew longer and more personal. We shared many deep and meaningful conversations. At times, a deep pain would surface when we spoke about family and love for others. I could feel it like it was my own, which makes perfect sense to me now. Maybe I brought that out of him, which Twin Flames will do. He was like no other I have ever met before, in this lifetime.

Still, I didn't realize what was truly happening until the last few days of his visit almost two years ago. That week I found myself unusually emotional, especially around the fact that his visit was shortly coming to an end and he would be returning home. I kept thinking why am I feeling so sad, it felt like something was shifting inside me and I couldn't name it yet. The morning before heading home, we decided to became friends on Facebook and even exchanged phone numbers, so we could stay in touch. I never thought I would hear from him so soon. That very afternoon he sent me a message that said, "I will miss our conversations in the morning." That sentence cracked something open. He later told me that during those final days he had felt something too, an overwhelming sense that something was different. Our souls were trying to tell us something.

Brian had been married for almost fifty years, and I was content in my marriage to Albert. Neither of us seeking anything beyond the lives we built. There was no intention, no pursuit, only a spiritual bond that awakened quietly, then powerfully. There was never a physical relationship between us, it was simply not written in the cards. What grew between us was a spiritual connection like anything I had ever known. A Twin Flame bond. It was a quiet knowing in the stillness between words. When we finally became aware of it the feeling was undeniable. Our conversations deepened, becoming more intimate, reflective and soul-stirring, as we were remembering something ancient and true.

The truth is it simply became too much to bear. As spiritually aligned as we were, our human selves struggled to carry the weight of it. It began to feel like a secret neither of us wanted to live with anymore. The connection was real, profound, soulful and sincere, but the situation was overwhelming, painful and complicated. Even the strongest soul connections can become too heavy for the heart to carry. Ours was real but it was never meant to stay.

We didn't speak for a week after that. Our last conversation was very brief, and I could hear sadness in his voice. I too was feeling the same, utterly heartbroken, but kept it together. As we said goodbye, I told him to look after himself and that I would always send prayers and love his way. It felt like I had been ripped open, like a deep wound left unattended and exposed. There were a couple of emails that followed, but neither of us had words for how we felt, so they came to a stop.

I cried every day for a long time and sank in a dark sadness. Nothing seemed to consol the pain. Even though it had lasted just a few months, the connection had been so powerful, so life-altering, that its absence left an echo I didn't know how to silence. He was the other half of my soul, and we knew each other better than we knew ourselves.

I was angry with Spirit for a while. I couldn't understand why I was brought to this point, why I had to experience something so intense, only to have it taken away. And why would I be brought this special person when I was already happily married? It felt cruel. We hadn't been looking for it, neither of us asked for it. And yet it found us, because on a soul level, it was all meant to be. It was part of our journey, our growth, and awakening.

I didn't tell Albert about him for a few months after stopping all communication with Brian. I explained I had crossed paths with someone who I believed to be my Twin Flame. I wouldn't say Albert was angry, but he was irritated and confused by it all. He was still trying to come to terms with the fact that I was communicating with Spirit, and this was something else entirely. He did seem a little thrown off by the Twin Flame concept. Truth be told, there were days I was still trying to grasp it. Still, I felt some relief after finally telling him, though part of me wished I had shared more, said it differently, and been able to help him understand what it truly meant for me on a soul level, in a way that didn't feel threatening to him.

Seven months ago, after a year of no contact, I felt a strong pull to reach out to Brian. I sent him a brief email to say hi and share a bit about what had been happening over the past year. I told him I missed him and could still feel him at times. He emailed back, saying he was doing OK and often thought about me and felt my presence. Even though our communication is limited, we still continue to connect through soul conversations. I often feel his presence around me and hear him call my name. We have even spoken to each other through dreams and synchronicities that reaffirm the deep bond we share through our combined energies, a kinship unlike any other. I'm learning to honor what we shared without the attachment of needing it to be something more.

Sometimes other Soulmate or soul connections can be just as intense as a Twin Flame connection, often mimicking the deep, magnetic pull that many associate with Twin Flames. So, you may ask: How would I know the difference?

Non-Twin-Flame Soulmate Connections are often deeply

loving, supportive, and harmonious. A Soulmate can be a romantic partner like Albert and me, or a close friend, or even a family member or pet. They enter our lives to help us grow, heal, and learn important lessons. While the connection is powerful, it is not always tumultuous or painful.

And then there are Karmic Relationships which can be intensely passionate but often come with cycles of pain, drama, and repeated lessons. They are meant to teach us something important but may not always last. Unlike a soulmate, a karmic relationship may feel draining rather than uplifting.

The key difference is how the connection makes you feel. Does it bring growth and healing, or does it feel like a never-ending emotional rollercoaster? Soulmate connections feel safe and natural, while Twin Flames often challenge you to the core. Karmic relationships, on the other hand, tend to be full of emotional highs and lows, with unresolved patterns repeating until the lesson is learned. I have experienced all of these.

It's important to trust your intuition and inner wisdom when determining the nature of your connection. Not every intense bond is meant to last forever, but each serves a purpose in your path of self-discovery and spiritual growth.

You are timeless, you are connected,
and you are never forgotten.

CHAPTER THIRTEEN

Feathers of Light—Embracing Messages from Above

Anyone who knows me understands how much I love feathers and how often I find them. I have collected so many that I share them with my friends. Feathers can be gifts from Angels, the Universe, or even a loved one conveying their presence and support. Finding a feather can be interpreted as a sign that you are being watched over and reminded to trust in your journey. When I find a feather, it's a gentle love letter from above, reminding me I am cherished.

"Feathers appear when angels are near."
— *Susan Heim*

Feathers can come in many different colors, mostly white, but I've also found blue, black, gray, even pink, or a combination of colors. I often discover them while out walking, underneath my big tree, but also inside my car, stuck in a door frame, and even backstage during a concert. Feathers continuously line my path, and I love them.

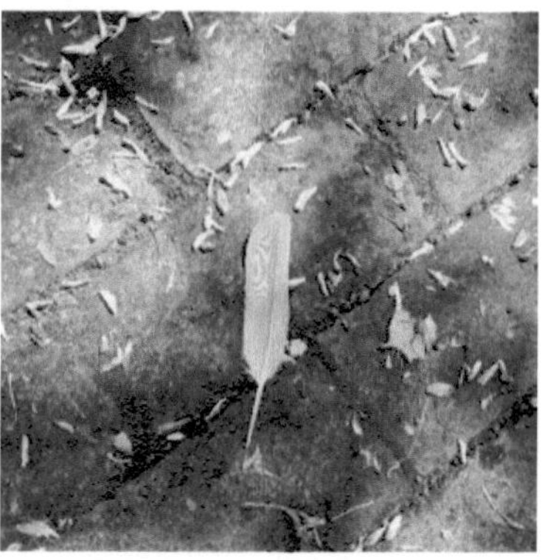

Found on the steps of a church

Found all these in a single day out walking

Here are a couple of my favorite stories about finding feathers. Last year, Albert and I took the dogs swimming in a nearby pond. They love to swim, so we take them as often as we can since summer is brief here in the Black Hills. As soon as I stepped out of the truck, I spotted a goose feather. I leaned down to pick it up and, when I looked across the field, I noticed feathers everywhere.

I found this backstage at a concert

This feather I found in my garden.

Albert suggested a goose was molting, shedding its winter coat. What was peculiar, though, was that each feather was individually placed evenly throughout the field. What a breathtaking sight! We collected a total of 155. I became very emotional and asked Spirit what it meant.

I heard, "It doesn't have to mean anything—just accept them as a gift."

How incredible is that?

Recently, I took two of my grandkids to Devils Tower in Wyoming. It's not far from where we live, a magical, spectacular place that can be seen from miles away. My grandkids know all about the significance of finding feathers, and they are always on the lookout for them. It was a cold day with a light snowfall, so I wasn't sure if we would find any, but we came across several small ones.

My granddaughter said, "I wish God would let us find a big feather."

I replied, "Maybe we will."

We all asked together. "Spirit, please, can you do that for us?"

As we walked a little farther, my granddaughter spotted a large magpie feather. It was divinely placed and perfect. I have never seen them so happy and filled with joy as when they found this one feather. I have that same feather framed as a keepsake that anything is possible, even when asking for a feather on a cold, snowy day.

Feathers can even bring you closer to someone, like my mum, who isn't particularly spiritual. Yet during what would unknowingly become my last visit with her, I found myself gathering feathers and carefully tucking them between the pages of a book. When my mum asked why I was doing all this, I told her they were gifts from Angels. She laughed lightly, brushing it off as merely birds molting and claiming it was just a coincidence that I found them. Yet the Christmas, before last, my oldest grandson, who loves birds, received an envelope from my mum filled with feathers. That moment brought me to tears, as I realized that the significance of feathers had truly resonated with her, and my mum had started collecting them.

Finding a feather is a kind of *"glimmer"*a fleeting or subtle sign, moment, or experience that provides inspiration, hope, or a sense of connection. Glimmers are often seen as a gift or message from the Universe or Spirit. They can manifest in various forms, such as finding meaningful objects (like heart-shaped rocks, or coins, or even buttons or hair ties).

Feather found at Devils Tower

I usually interpret these surprise gifts from Spirit as signs that say, "Hey, we love you! Keep up the good work."

Sometimes, I ask for a specific sign based on the answer I'm seeking, or just for fun. For example, once I requested to see a giant pink flamingo. It doesn't always happen right away when you ask, so give it time. To my surprise, a week later, my giant pink flamingo was sitting on a shelf at Walmart! I laughed out loud because Spirit has a sense of humor. Naturally, I had to take it home, and it sat in my office for a while until I gifted that beautiful pink flamingo to my youngest granddaughter as a gentle reminder that, "When you ask, you shall receive."

Then we have synchronicities: meaningful coincidences that occur when two or more events, ideas, or experiences align in a significant way.

I'm sure you've often encountered numbers repeating. The ones I commonly notice are: 111, 222, 333, 444, and 555, along with combinations like 1010, 1111, 1212, and even 1234. You may find that a particular number keeps appearing; these are indicators that signify Spirit is trying to get your attention. Some consider them Angel numbers. They validate that you're on the right path, or that your thoughts and intentions are being acknowledged or confirmed. Ultimately, it all comes down to what each number signifies for you personally. There are many books available that delve into the meanings of these numbers, if you wish to research further, but above all, ask Spirit directly and trust the answers you get.

Other synchronicities include coming across a book that answers a question you've been pondering, or meeting someone who shares a message that resonates deeply with your current situation. Or you might receive a sudden inner nudge or intuitive download that leads you to exactly what you have been seeking (a job, client, partner, or opportunity) that aligns perfectly with your desires or needs.

Unexpected connections occur when you randomly discover that a new acquaintance has a link to someone you've been thinking about or seeking advice from. My favorite synchronicities, which I seem to experience frequently, involve dreams. For instance, one night, you might have a vivid dream about a specific event or person, and shortly afterward, you encounter that event or person in real life.

Glimmers and synchronicities assure you that you are in tune with the Universe or your intuition. And whatever glimmer or gift you receive, it is a beautiful message from the heart that brings hope and serves as a reminder that you are loved. Your connection to Spirit is just a feather away.

As Emily Dickinson wonderfully stated, "Hope is the thing with feathers that perches in the soul and sings the tune without the words." This quote captures how hope can be gentle, uplifting, and readily present within us, much like a feather. It emphasizes that hope exists even in challenging times, often manifesting quietly but powerfully.

You are seen, you are heard, and you are deeply loved.

CHAPTER FOURTEEN

Light Language—The Voice of Your Soul

"The Soul speaks its own language that can only be understood by the heart."
— Unknown

Have you ever heard the voice of your Soul?

Earlier in this book, I shared how I spontaneously began speaking a different language. The church I attended called it receiving the Holy Ghost (or Holy Spirit) and speaking in tongues. I call it Light Language.

But regardless of what you call it, it is the voice of your soul, a deeply personal and spiritual expression that is uniquely yours. Many use Light Language for healing, believing it activates energies within the body, promotes spiritual transformation, and aligns you with your true self. Everyone has the ability to connect with this spiritual language; embracing it is a personal choice.

When do I use Light Language? When my mind feels occupied. When I'm seeking insight. When I need protection or healing. And when I am struggling to articulate emotions, I turn to this language to express what I'm experiencing. Often times, I don't understand the exact words I'm saying, yet I feel their power. Sometimes, my friend Jackie, who has the gift of translation, helps me interpret.

I also have discovered that I can express Light Language through hand movements and write it in symbols. Before I began to sign, I had no idea that it was even a thing. Then whether by chance, or guided by my inner compass, I stumbled across other kindred souls on YouTube who were signing it, too, each in their own way. Watching others express Light Language visually has further deepened my curiosity about the universal nature of these symbols and the messages and energy they seem to carry.

On many occasions, Light Language has served as a gateway to higher dimensions, allowing me to channel messages from realms beyond our own. I have spoken it during sessions or gatherings where Spirit has a message for all in attendance or for an individual. Because Light Language carries vibrational frequencies that resonate with our energy field and higher self, it is a direct link to the Divine.

One of my most profound experiences with Light Language occurred during a Winter Solstice celebration with friends. As we gathered in sacred space, I suddenly began speaking in the voice of a Lakota Medicine woman. Her essence flowed through me, even her rhythm, tone, and cadence carrying the wisdom of her lineage. The Light Language I spoke that day felt deeply rooted in the Earth's soil, infused with heritage, healing, and Spirit.

As her powerful energy surged through me, I channeled her messages, creating a profound sense of connection between our group and the spiritual realms. It was a moment of deep reverence and awakening, one that revealed how Light Language can transcend time and culture, bridging the seen and unseen worlds.

So, how do you find the voice of your soul? Sometimes, it is triggered by a powerful Spiritual event or emotional experience. Moments of deep connection, clarity, or joy can open the channel for this expression. I've also been told by Spirit that I can activate it in others, allowing them to access their own unique Light Language, similar to how a Reiki Master can activate higher levels of Reiki energy through a process called attunement.

What does Light Language sound like? It can resemble a foreign language, yet it feels otherworldly and transcendent. The rhythms, tones, and sounds don't follow familiar language patterns, making it a deeply spiritual experience. Sometimes, the language will flow through me with familiar sounds such as the Lakota, which holds a special connection to the Black Hills of South Dakota. Recently I spoke in what sounded like Chinese during a Past Life Reading. Other times, it sounds like Vulcan. Either way it's pretty cool and I love it.

I have several friends who speak Light Language but are still growing comfortable with using it in social settings. Others prefer to always keep it private. There are no rules. Your journey with Light Language is yours alone. During some of my sessions, I ask clients if they have ever felt an urge to speak in a different language. Many say yes but are unsure of what's happening. I'm grateful to help guide them through this experience, just as one day they may help others understand theirs.

The sound of Light Language varies widely from person to person, making it a highly individualized and fascinating way to connect to your Higher Self or the earthly and spiritual Realms I perceive Light Language as both your soul's voice and a way to receive divine healing and energy from highly evolved beings. Whether it's coming from inside of you or beyond you, it is a beautiful gift to cherish and share. I encourage you to explore your own Light Language and embrace this sacred connection with the Divine.

Whether expressed through sounds, symbols, or movement, all forms are valid. Experiment. Explore and let your voice and hands carry your soul's messages. Light Language not only supports your growth but can also inspire others.

There's no right or wrong way to connect with Light Language; it is a personal expression from deep within. Trust the process and let your journey unfold as you allow your Light Language to add to the greater light.

Nei Kaonei I shenei nako, oha, nei rahi hako neini rakona.
Na hossana kenei inei rako a nei reineri.
I nei rahoa kenei shenei tekini riushe nei rakoa.

Translation:
"I come not as a stranger, but as one who walks beside you.
The path has been long, but you have never been alone.
I bring the breath of remembrance, so you may
see clearly the power you carry within.

Stand in the truth of your heart, for it is
the light that guides nations."

"Naca une uskana."
Translation:

"You are loved."

CHAPTER FIFTEEN

Angels Who Walk Among Us

Have you ever crossed paths with an Angel? Would you recognize one if you did? The wings might be a giveaway, but the truth is, most of us wouldn't recognize an Angel even if we crossed paths with one. Yet, they walk (and fly) among us every day.

Angels exist on a higher frequency, their energy vibrating beyond our ordinary perception. As humans, we dwell in the third and fourth dimensions, where our vibrations are denser, making it challenging to sense their presence. To truly hear Angels, let alone see them, we must raise our own vibration, open our hearts, and attune our souls to their divine song.

I have had a couple of encounters with Angels. They have always stuck with me, and when I have moments of doubt, I remember these divine moments. They are subtle cues that I am never truly alone, that love and guidance are always near, even when unseen.

A couple of years ago, amidst the excitement of the Sturgis Motorcycle Rally, I experienced my first Angel moment. I was working in Deadwood, and part of my job was to monitor motorcycle parking on Main Street. This annual event draws over 750,000 bikers to the Black Hills, and though Sturgis (a small town just a few miles away) officially hosts the rally, it extends into surrounding communities such as Deadwood. My shift always began early, at 7 a.m., with the task of enforcing the city's parking ordinance, which prohibited parking on one side of the street until 10 a.m.

I'd cruise up and down Main Street in our loaned golf cart, taking the opportunity to chat with the bikers and answer their questions. The most frequent inquiry was always, "Where's a good spot for breakfast?"

Our local police chief had a humorous, yet candid response: "Home." It was clear he wasn't a fan of the chaos that came with the rally, which meant long days for him and his officers. I could certainly empathize with his sentiment, having had my own share of less-than-ideal encounters with bikers over the years.

One day, while I was parked in my rented golf cart a man walked up to me and asked a few questions about the town. He was in his late 50s, dressed in jeans, a white short-sleeved T-shirt, which was stained and soaked in sweat. His complexion was darker, and I noticed some teeth were missing. His hair was dark and messy. He had a rough, road-worn look, like someone who had been traveling a while and could use a shower, but there was a lightness in his voice and joy in his eyes. He spoke with a foreign accent I thought sounded like Hindu. He introduced himself as Sid. I remember his name vividly, as I had once been a punk rocker with a crush on Sid Vicious, so this made me smile. Only later did I learn the deeper connection, that Buddha's birth name was *Siddhartha.* That realization felt like one more confirmation that this man's presence carried spiritual weight that was beyond a mere human.

Sid didn't have a motorcycle. Instead, he had arrived in a white Suburban with only one working headlight. I sensed he was sleeping in his car. We ended up chatting for an hour, while I was trying to keep motorcycles from parking across the street.

He shared stories of his upbringing in India, speaking openly about his childhood and the hardships his family endured. He spoke with deep admiration of his father, who had worked tirelessly to save money so that he could travel to the United States in search of a better life. There was a sadness in Sid's voice, and tears welled in his eyes. Though they had been poor, he felt incredibly grateful because, in his words, he was now living the American dream.

Then he began to speak about his spiritual beliefs, thoughts on Hinduism, explaining how he saw the world as deeply interconnected through energy. He spoke of the divine presence in all living things and described the beauty of elephants, believing them to be sacred gifts from heaven.

I felt an undeniable resonance with him, as if we had met before in another time or place. Though we came from different backgrounds, there was something very special about him. I felt like there was a reason for this encounter and the wisdom he shared with me.

What happened next was nothing short of remarkable. Later that same morning, Albert called me and said he'd had a strange encounter with a man from India. He told me that this man had shown up at our house, asking about a car he had seen drive up our road. Our friends were in town and had brought their custom-built Rat Rod with them to drive around during the rally, a loud, gritty vintage-style car full of character, with exposed metal, and creative touches that turned heads whenever it went. It somehow caught the eye of the Indian gentleman. When Sid showed up at our home, he had expressed interest in learning more about this type of classic car. I guess he and Albert spoke for a while, and my oldest grandson really liked him and thought he was cool.

Albert said he was driving a white Suburban—with only one working headlight.

Now what are the odds?! I never told Sid anything about where I lived, and yet I knew it was him. The synchronicity sent chills down my spine, beyond mere coincidence—a divine meeting.

I spent the rest of the day seeking guidance from Spirit. "What was the significance of this meeting? What did this encounter mean?"

In the weeks following my encounter with Sid, I found myself asking Spirit if it was possible to catch another glimpse of an actual Angel. While I could already sense their presence, feel their energy around me, and hear their guidance, I longed for a visual confirmation, something tangible for my human eyes.

At times I would pause, and wonder: *Am I truly ready to see one?*

One night, I heard the verse again: *"Ask and you shall receive."*

Then came another quite unmistakable message: *"Angels walk amongst us."*

In that moment, understanding settled in. I realized Sid had been the answer all along. He had appeared before I even knew how to ask, before my conscious prayers had taken form. He did not look the way I had imagined an angel might, yet with every fiber of my being, I knew in a way that needed no explanation, that he was exactly what I had been meant to receive.

This also reminded me of the Bible passage:

"Do not forget to show hospitality to strangers,
for by so doing some people have shown hospitality
to Angels without knowing it."
— Hebrews 13:2

Since that day, I searched for Sid everywhere, hoping to see him again, but I never did. And perhaps that was the point, the gift already had been given.

What I did not yet understand was that the answer did not arrive just once. It continued to unfold quietly and unexpectedly through other encounters that followed.

Not long after meeting Sid, I had another encounter that stayed with me just as powerfully. I don't recall the man's name, but I will never forget his dog, Joker, a strong, muscular pit bull mix with a brindled, tortoiseshell coat and an unmistakably gentle presence. Joker had intelligent eyes and a calm steadiness that felt far beyond ordinary animal awareness.

The man himself was slim, likely in his early fifties, missing his lower teeth, and spoke softly. He smoked heavily and picked up odd jobs around town, doing some painting and handyman work, often at a local bar and grill. At first, I wondered if he and Joker were unhoused; he mentioned sleeping in his truck on more than one occasion. Yet there was nothing desperate about him. He carried himself with a quiet self-sufficiency, as though he and Joker were exactly where they needed to be.

The first time we met, Joker jumped straight into my lap as if he already knew me. There was no hesitation, no testing, just immediate recognition. Over the course of that summer, I saw them often while working on events around town: walking slowly down the street, sitting side by side on a bench, observing life rather than participating in it. Eventually, I started carrying dog treats in my pocket, just in case I crossed paths with Joker again.

I offered the man money once, wanting to help, but he declined gently, smiling as he told me they were doing just fine. There was something about the two of them that felt entirely outside the usual rhythms of life, calm, grounded, and quietly watchful. Being near them brought the same deep, unmistakable sense of divine presence I had felt with Sid. It wasn't dramatic or theatrical; it was subtle, steady, and profoundly peaceful.

What struck me even more was that Brian, without any prompting from me, shared his own encounter with the man and Joker during that same week. He described feeling different afterward, as if time slowed down, like something unseen had shifted within him, too. It mirrored my own experience so closely that it no longer felt coincidental. It was as though we were all moving through the same energetic corridor at once, connected by something beyond words.

Only later did I understand that this was also the week I began to recognize the depth of my connection with Brian, a bond I would eventually come to understand as Twin Flame.

Twins often share similar spiritual gifts and experiences because they mirror each other in many ways. Joker would jump into Brian's lap, just as he did with me. And I didn't see Joker doing that with anyone else. Almost every day, whenever Brian saw them, Joker would sit by his side, as if an unspoken bond existed between them. It was as though the dog recognized something within Brian, just as he had with me. I believe we all shared a deep soul family connection, and I interpreted this as a gentle reminder that Angelic Beings do indeed walk among us, often in the most unexpected ways, including the furry kind.

Looking back, it feels as though Spirit surrounded me during that time, offering confirmation through multiple forms: a stranger, a dog, a shared knowing, a quiet inner shift.

Whether the man and Joker were Angels, soul family, or divine messengers in another form, I cannot say with certainty. What I do know is how their presence changed me, and being near them brought a stillness, clarity, and sense of guidance that left a lasting imprint. Some encounters don't announce what they are. They simply arrive, do their work, and then quietly disappear, leaving you forever altered.

These crossings were far more than mere chance. They were signs that we are being guided, protected, and led toward deeper understanding—and the right connections at just the right time.

Perhaps you, too, have had moments like these, interactions that defy logic, leaving behind a deep and undeniable sense of the divine watching over you. Maybe you've heard stories of people surviving car accidents, feeling an unseen force holding them in place, or being shielded from harm. Some have reported seeing a bright light or felt an overwhelming sense of peace in the midst of chaos. There are even stories of people performing impossible feats, like lifting a car off someone trapped beneath it, or rescuing a drowning swimmer—only to vanish without a trace.

Divine happenings are all around us, often in the moments we least expect them. Sometimes, they come as a kind stranger with wise words, a fleeting conversation that leaves a lasting impact, or the unwavering love of an animal that seems to understand our soul. These connections are living proof that we are never truly alone. If we open our hearts and quiet our minds, we can begin to recognize the subtle ways the Universe whispers to us, through synchronicities, acts of kindness, and the inexplicable feeling of being exactly where we are meant to be.

Perhaps Angels don't always appear with wings and halos, but instead, they walk beside us in forms we recognize, offering love, guidance, and protection. All we have to do is pay attention and trust that we are divinely guided. Please enjoy the following poem I wrote about Angels and their loving presence all around us.

"Whispers of Angels"

They walk unseen in golden light,
A hush of wings, so soft, so bright.
Not always clad in robes of white,
But in a stranger's touch, so light.

A hand that lifts when you have fallen,
A voice that soothes when hope is gone.
A quiet whisper in the night,
A gentle push toward what is right.

Not all have halos, glowing fair.
Some wear the clothes of those who care.
A mother's song, a friend's embrace,
A fleeting glimpse of heaven's grace.

So when you feel alone or lost,
Or weary from the stormy cost,
Know Angels walk beside you still,
In love, in light, in quiet will.

— Sarah J. Kryger

CHAPTER SIXTEEN

Faith over Fear

"Faith over Fear" is a powerful mantra that emphasizes the importance of trusting in a positive outcome rather than succumbing to anxiety and doubt. It encourages us to focus on our beliefs, inner strength, and the assurance that, despite uncertainties, things can and usually do work out for the best. Faith can also be applied beyond spirituality; it involves trusting in people and ourselves, and trusting in the process, even in the face of uncertainty. Faith provides hope during challenging times, fosters resilience, and encourages us to pursue our goals with a deep inner belief that they will be achieved.

At its core, Faith is about embracing the unknown, maintaining a positive outlook regardless of circumstances, and having confidence in our beliefs, abilities, and values.

So why is it so hard to have Faith? Why is it so difficult to trust that everything will work out, and instead we allow Fear to take control? Even with all that has been shown to me, I still wrestle with choosing Faith over Fear. I believe this is only human.

Over the past year, I have been dealing with health issues. I realized I needed to make some changes in my life and that Spirit was urging me to take those necessary steps.

I was dealing with recurring bladder infections that never fully resolved, then, as a result of the antibiotics for the UTIs, I developed an ulcer. This wasn't my first ulcer; I had two previously. Back when I was working in a very stressful job, my doctor, who has treated me for over twelve years, warned me that stress can cause various health issues, including ulcers. At the time, I just laughed it off, knowing he was right, but not (yet) being willing to make the necessary lifestyle changes.

But this recent ulcer was the worst one ever, and if you've had one, you know how difficult it is to eat anything. It can be quite painful, and I was taking a lot of medication to reduce acid and coat my stomach. I decided to take a leave of absence and bought a ticket back home to England. The ulcer was so bad, I almost chose not to go. However, I turned everything over to Spirit and said, "I have no idea what to do. I need help." Thankfully, it started to heal, and I left for home a couple of weeks later.

Back in my homeland, I spent the first week alone before visiting my mum, and reconnecting with myself. So much had changed in my life since I had begun my spiritual awakening that I really didn't know who I was anymore. I needed this time to get to know myself better.

I walked a lot and visited places from my childhood, covering 5-10 miles each day. I explored old churches, old cemeteries, and even a castle. I spent time on the beach with my feet in the sand. I collected feathers, journaled about my experiences, and devoted a lot of time to praying and processing my emotions. It was a beautiful, Spirit-filled trip, and I felt an even stronger connection not only to myself but also to my mum.

Deep in my soul, I felt that something had shifted. I wasn't the same person I had been during earlier visits—I had awakened. There was more awareness, more softness, more truth within me. Spirit seemed to be guiding the whole experience.

Still, when I arrived, a wave of anxiety crept in, and I could sense a panic attack starting to emerge. I couldn't breathe and my chest was tight, so I headed to the bathroom where I attempted to pull myself together. Was my nervous system reacting to memories my mind had long buried? Maybe old energy, or even old roles from past lives? Whatever the cause, something cracked open in me. The visit became a mirror, showing me what still needed tending and who I had become in the process. Spirit was asking me to be fully present, not just with my mum, but with myself.

When I returned home, I realized I needed to decide whether to continue working at my current position as event coordinator. I loved my job and had been there for almost seventeen years, so this decision was difficult. At 58, I knew I wasn't getting any younger, and I felt a deep calling to change my life and follow a new path. It was a pivotal moment, requiring immense faith to move forward and trust that a greater plan was unfolding for me.

I recall coming across these words of wisdom by Mark Nepo, a remarkable author and spiritual teacher. "It may be that you find yourself in your 40s, 50s, or 60s and have just now awakened and become conscious of your life in many ways for the first time. Do not regret that this awakening didn't happen earlier in life. Your journey to this point will quickly be converted into wisdom that is invaluable for yourself and others. You are now embarking upon a personal renaissance—the zenith of your life. You are likely to find an acceleration of insight and understanding. You'll be figuring out certain things that would have taken twice as long just a few years ago. Let go of the past.

"What kind of life are you inspired to create for yourself? What is your heart telling you about your path forward? Have courage. Listen to yourself. Explore. Take a risk. This is your life. Take ownership of yourself. Cast off your concerns of what others think. Stop trying to please everyone else...."

"Maybe you're a late bloomer. Who cares?! Bloom! Don't allow the cultural narratives about age dictate how you think about yourself and the possibilities still ahead of you. Who says you can't direct and love your life? Don't hide your light. Be fearlessly authentic. This is what the world needs from you—you being you."

These words struck a deep chord with me, as I constantly felt (and still feel) like I'm running out of time. I am striving to cultivate a new perspective: that time is nothing but a clock on my wrist or wall or screen. I love this quote so much that I keep it displayed in my home office as a reminder that *being 58 or any age is not a limitation but a gift.* I often have passed along this message to others who feel they are too old to change their lives.

Initially, I planned to give my notice right away, but I waited another three months because it didn't feel like the right time. I needed to wait for and trust in divine timing. When I finally did submit my notice, I felt confident that I had made the right choice.

For the previous year and a half, I had been running my side business as a healer and intuitive—Yawning Dove—from home. Tracy recently purchased a space for her business, and now, after years of discussion, it was time to rent an office from her. Everything was finally coming together.

But this is where Faith over Fear truly comes into play. As I stood at the crossroads of my career, uncertain of what lay ahead, I kept coming back to another one of my favorite quotes:

"Faith is taking the first step even when you don't see the whole staircase."
— Rev. Martin Luther King Jr.

Faith isn't about having all the answers or knowing exactly how things will unfold; it's about trusting enough to take that first step. And then the next step. Baby steps and big leaps too.

And so, despite my fears, I stepped forward, trusting that Spirit had a plan for me. I turned in my three months' notice.

Walking away was emotionally difficult. I was so focused on freeing myself from time constraints that felt like an obstacle to my true calling as a healer that I hadn't fully considered how I would feel in the months that followed, even though I knew this was the right decision, and I felt Spirit's guidance every step of the way. Today I have no regrets about leaving, but at times, I miss the people I worked with for so many years.

This past month as I write this, I was once again asked to trust. Worried about my finances, I felt the need to find another job, so I asked Spirit to guide me toward a position that would be a good fit. Within a week, I came across an opening for a program coordinator at a local community center.

After a couple of interviews, it seemed like a good fit. I knew I had the experience and could help expand their reach in the community. Yet, deep down, something felt off. I felt like I was forcing myself to go through with it. Still, I accepted the position and, not listening to my intuition, I went in to complete the paperwork. The moment I stepped into the office, I was overwhelmed with anxiety and felt physically ill. Then, I noticed a feather lying on the floor in one of the offices, and suddenly, it hit me: *I can't do this. I don't want to.* The Angels were assuring me: "We are here, and you will be OK. Have faith." Without hesitation, I apologized and walked away.

I left feeling terrible, as though I had let them down—but also realizing that I had done this to myself by not listening to those initial gut warnings. I again heard: "Ask, and you shall receive." I had asked Spirit for a job, and I was given an option, even though deep down, I wasn't ready, and it wasn't the path meant for me. There are no wrong paths, but had I taken that job, I might have delayed what was truly planned for me. Sometimes an opportunity that appears is an chance for us to say no, to hone our intention and show the Universe, "Thanks, but no thank you. I know something even better is on the way!"

I've gained profound insight into the push and pull between Faith and Fear. At times, I've felt a deep certainty that everything is unfolding as it should. Other times, I've been consumed by doubt, afraid things won't go according to plan. It's a delicate balancing act between two opposing forces.

Ultimately, Faith over Fear is about trusting that everything is happening for our highest good, even when we can't see the full picture.

I've asked myself repeatedly: *What am I truly afraid of?*

Lately, my biggest fear has been whether I am on the right path, the one my soul is meant to follow. This fear has stirred deep emotions, revealing parts of myself that still need healing.

Yet, despite these fears, I remind myself that Faith requires surrender. Faith asks me to keep moving forward, and to believe that even in uncertainty, I am exactly where I need to be.

When we embrace Faith and Hope, especially in difficult times, we build resilience against Fear, and we empower ourselves, one choice at a time.

"Fear can banish Faith, but Faith can banish Fear."
— Billy Graham

You are divinely connected, always, in all ways.

CHAPTER SEVENTEEN

Simply Become Who You Are

I recently found a beautiful piece of framed artwork at a local thrift store that resonated deeply with me. It says, "Simply Become Who You Are," and features a stunning blue butterfly. This image holds special significance for me, as one of my Guides, Joseph Running Bear, often appears with a blue butterfly perched on his left shoulder. So of course I had to bring it home. It's hanging in my office, next to another sign that says: "Be grateful for what you have and proud of who you are." These messages keep me going some days and they nudge me to be present in the moment and appreciate the beauty in my life.

Like you, I've experienced my share of challenges and triumphs. Depending on the day and what's happening in my life, I need these subtle visual cues of my worth and accomplishments. My soul's journey has been a winding path, filled with highs and lows.

"Even the darkest night will end, and the sun will rise."
— Victor Hugo

I also believe that much of our path was set in motion long before we were born. I was born to experience it all: the pain, the hurt, the sadness, the joy, the peace, the freedom, and above all, the love. I was meant to shine in many roles: as a daughter, granddaughter, mother, grandmother, wife, and proud dog mom. My journey has been extraordinary, with its fair share of twists and turns. I had an incredible career in radio, one that began by chance but became a true passion. Then for the next seventeen years, I thrived as an event coordinator, organizing and running large-scale events. Along the way, I met incredible entertainers and worked alongside truly amazing people, each walking their own path and each one a unique Beautiful Soul.

It can be difficult to grasp, but our soul chooses to engage and learn in this lifetime, perhaps even as a second chance if we didn't succeed in the last. In doing so, we carry forward emotions and what I like to call a "template." For me, this template revolves around having Faith while struggling with financial uncertainty and worries about not following my soul's true path. Learning to truly love myself and find comfort in being alone is an ongoing journey, yet a priority for me.

Lately, I've noticed that some of my friends are no longer seeking a significant other; instead, they're embracing their time alone or cherishing moments with their children and family. They're completely at peace with this choice, and I feel their Faith has grown stronger as a result. Ultimately, our soul longs to find contentment in the present, realizing that fulfillment doesn't always come from outside sources but from within. This helps us remember that *true strength and peace come from fully embracing ourselves, trusting our journey, and knowing we're whole on our own.*

So, who am I, and who am I meant to be?

For me, it comes down to trusting that what's meant for me will always arrive on time— and not human time, either, but divine time.

I'm trusting my intuition and aligning with my true calling as a healer. Every morning, I ask Spirit to give me the opportunity to help someone that day. Ironically, I've found it's often easier to help others see their path than it is to recognize my own, and I've come to accept that. Just as I support others, I also seek guidance when I need clarity on my own journey.

Throughout my spiritual awakening, I've learned a great deal about myself, my personality, my likes and dislikes and I've come to accept that it's OK to change. I've recently come to realize that some pleasures I once enjoyed no longer bring me happiness, and that certain relationships that were once important no longer serve me. Some have been difficult to let go of, while others have been surprisingly easy to release as I've come to recognize my true worth.

Over time, I've let go of deep-seated trauma and pain. In doing so, I'm a step closer to who I'm meant to be.

Our journey isn't about becoming someone new.

It's about remembering who we truly are.

The little girl from England has grown in so many ways. If I could go back and speak to her, I would say: "Sweet girl, you are stronger than you know. Life will test you, and there will be moments when you feel lost, but I promise you are never alone.

You are deeply loved, guided, and protected. Every challenge you face will shape you into the incredible, radiant soul you are meant to be. Hold on to your Faith, trust your journey, and never dim your light for anyone. One day, you'll look back and see that every step, even the painful ones, led you to something greater. Keep shining, keep believing, and know that you are enough—just as you are."

If you could send a message back in time to your past self, what would you tell them? You may want to write these words of compassion down in your journal or even send yourself a love letter or card. You can also just imagine doing this as an inner visualization.

Becoming who you truly are is about unlearning, accepting, and allowing. It's not so much about becoming as it is about revealing and shedding the expectations, fears, and conditioning that shaped you but don't define you. It means leaving the past behind and focusing on the path ahead.

My path of remembering who I am is a continuous journey, and each day, I learn a little more about myself. Spirit guides me to stay true to who I am and to stand confidently in the power that is rightfully mine. I am learning to overcome fear, move forward with grace, and serve others with the same compassion I offer myself.

I don't see myself as anything special. In fact, I'm just an ordinary person navigating my spiritual path, facing life's challenges, learning, and growing just like everyone else. I get angry sometimes if things aren't going my way, and sometimes I even get mad at Spirit. I ask Spirit for guidance and for signs every day, and sometimes I cry myself to sleep or just cry for no reason. Not for the past or present, just because I am grateful to Spirit for loving me and giving me hope that all will work out and that I am a Beautiful Soul.

But perhaps the greatest journey of all has been learning to accept the changes within me. Who I was is no longer an option; what matters is who I am at this moment.

And at this moment, I am whole.

As we get ready to conclude this journey together, I want to share with you an uplifting message of encouragement and empowerment. You are a unique and radiant being, carrying and carried by a soul filled with wisdom, love, and infinite potential.

Honor your true self, your uniqueness, imperfections—everything that makes you who you are. Your path is yours alone, and no one else can walk it quite like you. While others may share similar experiences, your journey of self-discovery and spiritual growth is uniquely your own. Trust yourself. Trust the process.

Be gentle with yourself as you navigate life's twists and turns. Even when uncertainty arises, and your faith is tested, remember that you are exactly where you need to be, and everything is unfolding as it should. The Universe has a way of guiding you, even when you cannot yet see the full picture. Listen to your intuition, for it is the truth of your soul.

What works for others may not work for you, and that's OK. Honor your inner knowing, for it holds the guidance you seek. May you continue to listen to the whispers of your soul and trust in the wisdom of your heart.

Above all, know that you are loved and supported, always. You have a team of spiritual Angels and Guides who are here to help you. Take the time to get to know them, ask questions, trust they have your best interest at heart, and they have your back.

You are never alone on this journey, Beautiful Soul. We are in this together.

I leave you with this final thought:

"You were born with potential. You were born
with goodness and trust. You were born with
ideals and dreams. You were born with greatness.
You were born with wings. You are not meant for crawling,
so don't. You have wings. Learn to use them and fly."
— Rumi

You are becoming, you are remembering,
and you already are everything you need.

EPILOGUE

The Essence of Energy

This chapter was not originally part of my book; it came to life after my friend Tosha read my manuscript and brought back countless moments I had shared with her over the years. I was amazed by how much she remembered. In many ways, she has become the keeper of my story, woven into both my path and this book.

In many ways, this feels like the perfect time to write this chapter on energy as this past week has been especially emotional. I've spent much of it in tears, seeking comfort and guidance from my Angels and Spirit Guides. I've asked for their support in making sense of the energy I felt and also allowing myself to fully experience and express my emotions as they come.

Recently I attended a Spirit Expo, where I had the opportunity to offer readings for others. I love connecting through my

Tarot deck, allowing Spirit to guide me in sharing messages, and I often pick up on various energies and deeply feel them, making each reading a deeply personal and powerful experience.

As an empath, I naturally feel others' emotions deeply, especially when they receive a message from a loved one or share their personal stories. I connect with them on a profound level, experiencing their sorrow and pain as if it were my own. I've spoken with others who have faced similar challenges, and I know that maintaining energetic boundaries is important. While I try to be mindful of protecting my own energy, distancing myself can be difficult, and it's easier said than done if you are empathic.

I have touched on the concept of energy throughout several chapters of this book, but it truly deserves a chapter of its own. Energy is the essence of everything, and we are all energy, interconnected in ways beyond what we can see. The very force that sustains life, the rhythms of the Universe, and the pulse of the planet itself all exist as energy.

I came across a scientific experiment that demonstrated how our intentions and emotions can influence water and ice. Dr. Masaru Emoto's groundbreaking work, now detailed in his bestselling book, *The Hidden Message in Water,* explored this phenomenon by photographing frozen water crystals after they had been exposed to different words, thoughts and emotions. His research suggested that simply holding a glass of water and expressing gratitude can actually alter its crystalline structure.

Water, in its ever-changing and flowing nature, responds to energy, whether in the form of thoughts, words, images, or vibrations. This resonated with me, so I decided to try it for myself. As I held the glass of water in my hands, I focused on gratitude and intention. Almost instantly, I felt warmth in my hands, followed by a gentle tingling sensation, much like the energy flow I experience when practicing Reiki. Proof that energy is not just something around us; it is within us, responding to our thoughts and emotions, shaping our reality in ways we may not always consciously perceive.

Now let's explore other forms of energy, such as portals. Most of the portals I've heard about were opened unintentionally, allowing various energies to pass through. You may have seen them portrayed in stories that later become movies and often depicted as mysterious or even ominous doorways used by wizards like Merlin or other mystical beings to cross into other worlds, dimensions, or universes.

In reality, these energetic doorways really can connect different realms or dimensions, and when left unchecked, they may invite unexpected spiritual energies. I believe portals also can naturally appear or open in places with high-vibrational energy, such as in nature (tree or rock archways, waterfalls) or can be enhanced and honored with human designs at sacred sites like Stonehenge and other stone circles. I have seen and felt the power of portals a couple of times at Devils Tower in Wyoming and often at Pathways Spiritual Sanctuary near Lead, South Dakota.

A couple of years ago, during a visit to Pathways with Tracy, as we walked, I stepped through what I now call an energy portal or gateway. The sensation was so intense I nearly passed out. It was like a sudden burst, a tingling rush of energy moving through my whole body. Thankfully Tracy was right beside me, and she felt it too. Since then, I have encountered similar surges on later visits, but never quite as powerful as the first time. I believe Spirit was showing me something in that moment, something meant to wake me up.

We, too, are energy, and our own elevated vibrations can create or access these gateways, both positive and negative. This is why understanding energy portals is so important and becoming aware of the unseen forces around us allows us to navigate them with intention and caution.

Before choosing to explore any portal, it's essential to recognize the potential effects and to ensure you are energetically prepared for what may come through or what you may experience there.

During one intuitive energy session, I encountered something unusual on my client's shoulder. Every time I placed my hands over the area, I felt a strange pull, almost as if something were trying to draw my hands in. It was an odd sensation, and I kept being drawn back to that same spot. Unsure of what I was dealing with, I turned to Spirit for guidance, asking for clarity on what this energy was and how to address it.

Spirit informed me that it was, in fact, a portal and that it needed to be closed. The client had accidentally opened one, though I had no idea why it was located on her shoulder. I immediately focused on closing it, asking for continued guidance on how to do so. Spirit instructed me to simply place my hands on it and set the intention to close the portal. I did close the portal, but I never mentioned it to the client, as I felt she might be concerned or not fully understand, and I didn't entirely understand it myself at the time. This was a powerful lesson, making me more aware that portals can exist anywhere, sometimes without us even realizing it.

In addition to through portals, energy can enter your body in various forms, for example, through an angelic presence or even an Ancestor. While reading for a Native American woman at a Spirit Expo, I met one of her Ancestors, an incredibly powerful medicine man. His presence was undeniable. I could feel his energy surrounding her as I read her cards. The moment I spoke of him, an intense sensation washed over me, and I no longer felt alone. Suddenly, I experienced something entering my body, and before I knew it, I was speaking in his language, delivering messages that only she could understand. She recognized the language and spoke of this medicine man, sharing how she often sensed a presence around her. When I mentioned his name, White Horse, a spark of recognition lit up her face as though it confirmed what—and who—she had been sensing.

*"Three of my grandchildren at Pathways Sanctuary,
a magical land where my grandkids and I
all sensed energy and portals in several places."*

After delivering White Horse's message, the medicine man's presence left my body, and both my client and I sat in amazement, overcome with emotion. The air felt electric as his energy was still lingering between us. Heat gathered at the back of my neck, and I began to sweat. My heart pounded, adjusting to the shift back into the physical world.

Tracy, at a booth next to mine, sensed the shift in energy and asked, "What just happened?"

The experience was profound and humbling, a great example of the deep spiritual connections we share with our Ancestors.

However, it took me some time to fully clear his energy. I felt shaky and had to step away to process what had just occurred. Though I never felt fear, I knew I needed to be more mindful moving forward. It became clear to me that while these spiritual encounters can be incredibly moving, I must ensure that such things only happen with my permission.

These are just a couple of examples of how powerfully energy can present itself at any time and how we as energy beings can explore different spiritual dimensions, deepen our connections with the unseen world, and even facilitate healing and transformation.

Energy is not just something we feel; it is something we interact with, intentionally or unintentionally, in ways that shape our journeys and perceptions.

"Energy flows where intention goes" is a phrase often used by motivational speaker Tony Robbins, but its origins trace back to Huna philosophy, an ancient Hawaiian tradition. This concept highlights the power of focus and intention because wherever we direct our thoughts and energy, we initiate movement and transformation in our lives.

You are pure energy, you are eternal light, and you are love embodied.

AFTERWORD

A Message from My Heart

I want to thank you from the depths of my heart for walking beside me. Sharing these stories and revisiting my past has invited me into some uncomfortable spaces, but it has been very healing. If there's one thing I hope you take away from this book, it's this:

Healing is possible, no matter where you begin.

Life is not meant to be perfect. It is messy, beautiful, painful, and magical, and it's always unfolding. At times I questioned my worth, my purpose, even my very existence.

But God never left me.

And I want you to know: God has never left you either.

You are never too broken, too far gone, or too lost to find your way back to the light.

Your soul remembers who you are, even when you forget.

The healing path is not linear, and it's not always smooth, or even comprehensible.

But it is significant, empowering, and very personal.

Whether you feel called to work with Spirit, to explore your past lives, or simply to sit quietly and listen to your heart, I invite you to trust the whispers of your soul. Trust that the journey you are on is uniquely yours and that you are being guided, even when it feels like you're standing still.

You are a divine being, here on Earth to learn, remember, and love. I pray that my story helped you tap into your own inner wisdom and inspired you to keep going, keep glowing, and keep showing up for yourself.

Take one day, one breath, one moment of love at a time.

Thank you for seeing me, for holding space for my truth, and for allowing me to be a part of your path. May you continue to walk with faith, courage, and the unshakable knowing that you are never truly alone.

With All My Love, Sarah

APPENDIX

Affirmations for Your Heart and Soul

I am seen, I am worthy, and I belong.

✳

I am held, I am nurtured, and I am never alone.

✳

I am on the right path, and the signs are all around me.

✳

I am rising, I am reclaiming, and I am powerful.

✳

I am loved beyond time, and love never truly dies.

✳

I am awakening, I am expanding, and I am Light.

✳

I have a direct line to Spirit, and I receive divine messages.

✳

I matter, I am special, and I am deeply loved.

✳

I am gifted, I am guided, and my presence is a blessing.

✳

Forgiveness is a sacred gift I give myself and to others.

✳

I am surrounded, I am protected, and I am cherished.

✳

I am seen, I am heard, and I am deeply loved.

✳

I am timeless, I am connected, and I am never forgotten.

✳

I am divinely connected—always, in all ways.

✳

I am becoming, I am remembering,
and I already have everything I need.

I am pure energy, eternal light, and love embodied.

I am a beautiful soul.

ABOUT THE AUTHOR

Sarah Kryger is the mother of two and grandmother of four, a role that brings deep meaning and joy to her life. She lives in the beautiful Black Hills of South Dakota, where nature inspires and nurtures her soul.

Her personal journey through trauma, healing, and spiritual awakening guided her to share her story here in *Called by Spirit: Becoming Sarah—A Spiritual Memoir of Light and Resilience,* her first book. Sarah is a psychic medium, past-life regression hypnotherapist, and spiritual intuitive. With a heart-centered approach, she offers guidance, healing, and insight to help others reconnect with their higher selves and the wisdom within. Sarah provides intuitive readings, energy healing, and past-life insights, creating sacred spaces for clarity, transformation, and peace. She shares her home with her husband, Albert, their two loyal labradors, Duke and Alice, and a rescued dove named Pidgy Widgy, the mascot for her business name: Yawning Dove. Sarah draws her strength from Spirit and finds comfort in knowing she is never truly alone.

Duke and Alice

Pidgy Widgy

If you were touched by this book, please consider:
Sharing the link to the book, or the author's website.
Leaving a review on Amazon to boost the book's visibility.
Donating a copy to a library, women's or homeless shelter, community or spiritual center.
Thank you!

ACKNOWLEDGMENTS

First, I want to give special thanks to God, my Father in Heaven, and to my Angels and Spirit Guides who have been by my side throughout my life. Through every twist and turn, every heartache and tear, they quietly carried me, even when I didn't yet know they existed. Their presence has been my grounding force, my comfort, and the quiet whisper that keeps me moving forward. I have never felt more loved.

To my mum, who I know can hear me, from "the other side," because there is no separation when it comes to love: Our relationship wasn't always easy. We walked a complex path together, and I'm so glad that we grew closer while we still had time. I've come to love and appreciate you deeply. I honor the journey we shared and the lessons it's brought. You will always be a part of my soul's path, and I'm so grateful for the bond we shared and for the one that will continue in Spirit. Thank you for giving me life, for being a part of my life, and for helping shape the woman I've become. I know I walk forward with a blessing from an Angel by my side.

To my nan and granddad, who gave me the gift of unconditional love. In their presence, I always felt safe, cherished, and truly seen. Though they too have passed on, I still feel their presence near, always guiding me with love and grace.

To my children, Jillian and Jason, and my wonderful grandchildren, Oliver, Raelynn, Carter, and Ivy: You bring joy, happiness, and fulfillment to my life.

To my husband, Albert: You have remained steadfast by my side with unwavering love and quiet support, even as I transformed before your eyes. As I have evolved spiritually, emotionally, and soulfully, you never questioned, only loved. With an open heart and open mind, you embraced every shift in me. Your presence has been my anchor through the winds of change, and your belief in me has given me the strength to become who I was always meant to be.

To my best friend and soul sister Tracy: Thank you for being a bright light since the very beginning of my spiritual awakening. You've carried me through the highs and lows, through the shadows and the light. When I faltered, you reminded me of my inner power. When I doubted, you reminded me who I was. One step at a time, you gently nudged me forward. You've been my rock, and the steady grace beside me. Our sisterhood goes far beyond this lifetime, and I am endlessly grateful to journey beside you in this one.

To my beloved friends:

Dawn, thank you for believing in me from the beginning. Your excitement and curiosity about my spiritual journey made me feel seen and supported, and your steady presence helped bring this book to life. Tosha, Ashley, and Melody. Thank you for believing in me from the very beginning of my awakening. Your excitement and curiosity about my spiritual path made me feel seen and anchored. Your presence has illuminated these words. When I felt small, you lifted my gaze to my wings.

Bobby, thank you for nearly thirty years of friendship that began during my radio days and grew into something steady and rare. Your unwavering support, honesty, and presence have meant more to me than words can fully express.

David Borsh, thank you for your generous sponsorship and endless support. I appreciate your kindness more than words can say.

With gratitude to my editor, Sage Taylor Kingsley, whose intuitive guidance and editorial wisdom shaped this book with clarity and heart.

David Provolo, thank you for the beautiful cover and interior design. Your work elevated this book in ways I deeply appreciate.

To all my dearest friends and family: Thank you for never doubting me, for being by my side through every shift, and for gently cheering me on to embrace my soul's purpose.

From the depths of my soul, thank you all.

You are my Earth Angels, and your light has helped guide me.

EMERGENCY SUPPORT & RESOURCES

If you are or someone you love is struggling with thoughts of suicide, abuse, or emotional distress, please know that help is available. You are not alone, and there are people who care and want to help you.

Emergency Support (United States)
National Suicide & Crisis Lifeline
📞 988 (Call or Text)
www.988lifeline.org
Free and confidential support 24/7.

National Domestic Violence Hotline
📞 1-800-799-SAFE (7233) or Text "START" to 88788
www.thehotline.org
Aid for those affected by domestic violence or abuse.

RAINN (Rape, Abuse & Incest National Network)
📞 1-800-656-HOPE (4673)
www.rainn.org
Advocacy for survivors of sexual abuse and assault.

If you're outside of the United States, please reach out to a local crisis center or emergency services in your area. Compassionate assistance is always within reach.

You are not alone. You are worthy. You are deeply loved.

OTHER RECOMMENDED RESOURCES

Dolores Cannon—A Pioneer in Past-Life Regression and Consciousness Exploration
Book: *The Search for Sacred Hidden Knowledge*
www.dolorescannon.com

A.L. Garris—Light Language Intuitive
Book: *AQE Foundations: Remember Who You Are*
www.sacredexpansion.com

Mark Nepo—Poet and Spiritual Philosopher
Book: *The Book of Awakening*
www.marknepo.com

Theresa Caputo—Television Personality and Psychic Medium
Book: *There's More to Life Than This*
www.theresacaputo.com

Edgar Cayce—One of the Most Documented Psychics in History
Book: *There is a River* by Thomas Sugrue
Edgar Cayce's Association for Research and Enlightenment
www.edgarcayce.org
Dani Jo—Psychic Medium
Book: *Illuminate the Dark*
www.psychicmediumdanijo.com

Tracy Island, CHT—Hypnotherapist and Healer
Guides clients through spiritual growth, by releasing past traumas, healing the inner child, integrating past life wisdom, and harmonizing divine feminine and masculine energies.
www.calmingwavehypnosis.com

Ashley Sanders—Astrologer, Holistic Yoga Teacher and Daoist Stone Medicine Practitioner
www.halcyoncreatives.com

Book: *Pocket Guide to Spirit Animals* by Dr. Steven D. Farmer
A compact and insightful reference book about the meaning and messages of spirit animals.
www.drstevenfarmer.com

Book: *Spirit Animal Directory* by Dawn Baumann Brunke
A helpful resource for understanding the wisdom and guidance of spirit animals.

TAROT DECKS:

Rider-Waite Tarot Deck by Arthur Edward Waite
Angel & Spiritual Oracle Decks by Kyle Gray
Spirit Cards Oracle Deck by John Moseley
The Dream Song Oracle by Angi Sullins
The Light Seer's Tarot by Chris-Anne

The Sound Pillow Sleep System
www.soundpillow.com

And last but not least, please explore my website
to learn more about my healing work,
psychic mediumship, and Light Language sessions:

www.YawningDove.com

www.ingramcontent.com/pod-product-compliance
Ingram Content Group UK Ltd.
Pitfield, Milton Keynes, MK11 3LW, UK
UKHW040150310726
14061UKWH00006BB/199/J